The Dividend Clientele Hypothesis:
Evidence from the 2003 Tax Act

Laura Kawano[1]
March 2011

Abstract

In this paper, I test the dividend clientele hypothesis (DCH) by examining the impact of the Jobs and Growth Tax Relief Reconciliation Act of 2003 (the 2003 tax act) on household portfolio dividend yields. The DCH predicts that the 2003 tax act, which reduced the tax-disadvantage of dividends differentially across the income distribution, would cause high income households to shift their portfolios towards dividend paying stocks relatively more than lower income households. Using the 2001 and 2004 Surveys of Consumer Finances (SCF), I examine how changes in tax rates affect changes in household portfolio dividend yields. I find that the 2003 tax act caused households in the highest (35%) tax bracket to increase their portfolio dividend yields by 1.1 percentage points more than those in the next (33%) tax bracket, and by 2.6 percentage points more than those two tax brackets (28%) below. Compared to a 2.1 percent average dividend yield in 2001, these responses are large and economically significant. Using the 2007 SCF, I find that the reduced variation in dividend tax rates across households caused portfolio dividend yields to become homogeneous within three years of the tax act. Using a battery of sensitivity checks, I verify that these findings are not driven by other explanations for changes in dividend preferences, such as changes in optimism or risk-aversion.

---

[1] This paper was primarily written while I was a graduate student at the University of Michigan. I am grateful to my dissertation committee members, Amy Dittmar, Matthew Shapiro, Joel Slemrod and Jeff Smith for invaluable guidance, to Kevin Moore for assistance with using the Survey of Consumer Finances data, and to Daniel Feenberg for assistance with the NBER TAXSIM model. Charlie Brown, Jim Hines, Sara LaLumia, Sebastien Bradley, Josh Cherry, Osborne Jackson, Ryan Nunn, Todd Pugatch, and participants at the University of Michigan public finance and labor seminars, various colleges and government agencies, and the 2007 Midwest Economics Association Annual Meetings provided useful feedback. Additional comments can be sent to laura_kawano@treasury.gov.

1 Introduction

Because dividends and capital gains generally face different tax rates and these rates vary across individuals, an equity security provides different after-tax returns for individuals facing different tax rates. Miller and Modigliani (1961) hypothesize that such heterogeneity leads to what they termed a "dividend clientele effect": investors naturally sort into equity holding classes based on their dividend payout ratios. According to the dividend clientele hypothesis, firms with high (low) dividend-payout ratios attract investors with low (high) marginal tax rates. In the aggregate, an individual's portfolio dividend yield, i.e., the ratio of dividend income to the value of equity holdings, should decrease with income.

This paper examines the dividend clientele hypothesis by analyzing the response of household equity portfolios to the Jobs and Growth Tax Relief Reconciliation Act of 2003 (henceforth referred to as the 2003 tax act). There are two major components of the 2003 tax act. First, capital gains tax rates were reduced. Second, dividend income was now taxed at the same rates as capital gains, rather than ordinary income. Together, these changes greatly reduced the tax disadvantage of dividend income and, importantly, did so by a relatively larger amount for high-income individuals. By providing exogenous variation in marginal tax rates, the 2003 tax act provides an opportunity to examine the dividend clientele hypothesis in a natural experiment framework.

This paper has two goals. The first is to test whether the relationship between tax rates and household portfolio choices is consistent with the dividend clientele hypothesis. There are previous empirical studies that examine dividend clientele effects. This study contributes to this existing literature both in terms of the quality of data used and empirical methodology employed to provide a more compelling estimate of the causal impact of taxes on household portfolio dividend yields. I use data from the Federal Reserve Board's 2001, 2004 and 2007 Surveys of Consumer Finances (SCF), a triennial survey that contains detailed information on household wealth. Importantly, the SCF data allow accurate marginal tax

1

rate calculations and a rich description of portfolio structures, the combination of which is not common to other data sources. In addition, the timing of the 2003 tax act clearly separates tax regimes across the SCF samples. I exploit the resulting exogenous variation in tax rates to identify tax effects rather than relying on variation in a single cross-section. This paper is the first to test for dividend clienteles among the class of individual investors using a natural experiment.

The second goal is to quantify the clientele-related economic impact of the 2003 tax act. Because the supply of dividends also changed, this paper is related to earlier studies of firm responses to the 2003 tax act that document the increase in dividend payments (Chetty and Saez (2005), Brown, Liang and Weisbenner (2004)). Note, though, that the overall supply of dividends increased does not inform how these dividends were distributed across households. This question can only be answered by directly considering changes to household portfolios, as is done here.

The paper addresses two econometric issues. First, the dependent variable, a household's portfolio dividend yield, has a mass point at zero. Second, the main regressor of interest, tax rates, is endogenous to investor choices. To account for these issues, I estimate a Tobit-type model with instrumental variables techniques. The natural experiment framework provides an instrumental variable that is preferable to those used in previous research designs. Specifically, the different intensities of tax treatment that households face provides the basis for separating households into low- and high-treatment groups used to identify the effects of taxes.

I find strong evidence for the dividend clientele hypothesis. I estimate that the relationship between the tax disadvantage of dividend income and household portfolio dividend yields is negative and statistically significant. This suggests both that taxes cause a high degree of investor sorting and that households quickly responded to the tax changes caused by the 2003 tax act. In particular, affluent households shifted their portfolios, either actively or passively, to high dividend yielding stocks in response to the 2003 tax act. I also find that in the longer term, portfolio dividend yields became quite similar across households. This finding is expected because the distributions of effective dividend and capital gains tax rates were compressed. The differences between the short-term and longer-term responses are interesting and informative regarding the heterogeneity in portfolio adjustments and the importance of adjustment costs.

To assess the economic impact of the 2003 tax act, I use the parameter estimates to simulate the change in portfolio dividend yields caused by the 2003 tax act. I find that households in the top tax bracket more than doubled their portfolio dividend yields (a 115% increase). These top tax bracket households increased their yields by 1.1 percentage points more than those households in the next tax bracket and by 2.6 percentage points more than those two tax brackets below, reflecting the relative intensity of the tax treatment. In addition, the 2003 tax act caused a 0.94 percentage point differential response in portfolio dividend yields across treatment groups, defined by educational attainment measures. Given that average portfolio yields in the 2001 SCF were 2.05%, this represents a large and economically significant response.

I run a battery of specification tests to verify that the estimated response to the 2003 tax act is not explained by other factors. I determine that the estimates are robust to different treatment group definitions, to different outlier cut-offs, and to alternative methods of handling imputed values. I find that the main conclusions are unchanged when relaxing the assumptions of the Tobit model. I check that other determinants of household preferences for dividends, such as expectations over the future performance of the economy, did not change differentially across treatment groups over the two periods considered.

Understanding the relationship between taxes and investor decisions is important for several reasons. First, such information is useful to corporate financial managers who may consider the tax characteristics of their investors to determine optimal financial policies.

Second, because equity holdings and dividend receipts have historically been concentrated in the upper tail of the income distribution, the impact of changing tax rates on household equity portfolios has important implications for the redistributive properties of the tax system. Indeed, one argument for taxing dividend income at higher rates than capital gains has been that it aids the progressivity of the tax schedule. Lastly, the magnitude of household behavioral responses to changes in the tax structure inform estimates of the efficiency losses of taxation (Galper, Lucke and Toder 1988). For example, the relationship between taxes and portfolio choice is central to tax reform discussions because switching to a comprehensive income tax or a consumption tax would eliminate the differential tax treatment of assets. Because reorganizing investment strategies can be costly, understanding shifts caused by changing tax rates is important to such debates.

The remainder of the paper is organized as follows. Section 2 reviews theoretical models of dividend clientele formation. Section 3 summarizes the main components of the 2003 tax act. The data and methodology are described in Section 4. Section 5 provides a presentation and discussion of the results, while section 6 concludes. Appendix A provides a brief overview of a related line of research regarding dividend clienteles, and Appendix B provides detailed descriptions of the sensitivity checks for the main analysis.

2   Theory of dividend clienteles

The Modigliani-Miller theorem establishes that in perfect capital markets (i.e., without taxes, transaction or bankruptcy costs, or asymmetric information) a firm's dividend policy does not affect its value (Modigliani and Miller 1958). In this setting, investors can replicate any stream of dividend payments through the purchase and sale of appropriate equities. Thus, investors view dividend polices as irrelevant and will not pay a premium for any particular policy. However, when investors face different dividend and capital gains tax rates, they have different after-tax valuations for the same asset. Miller and Modigliani hypothesize that such differences lead to the formation of what they termed "dividend clienteles," in which investors have tax-based preferences over equities that differ only in their dividend policies (Miller and Modigliani 1961).

To gain intuition for the mechanism through which investor clienteles emerge, I apply Miller's (1977) simple clientele model to the case of dividend policies. For simplicity, assume that there are two available stocks: one that does not pay dividends and one that does. Both stocks are assumed to be riskless and there is no available debt security. Also assume that the tax rate on capital gains (τ_{cg}) is zero, while the tax rate on dividend income (τ_{div}) increases with income. The market equilibrium of this model is depicted in Figure 1.

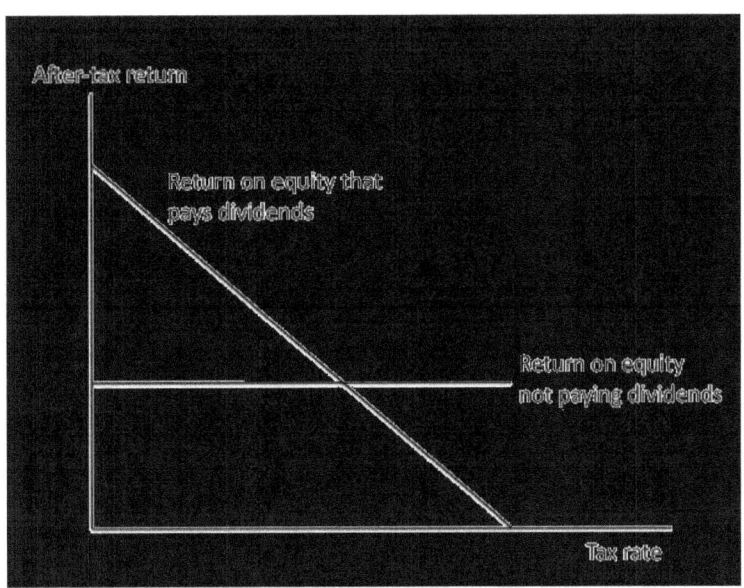

Figure 1: Equilibrium in the Miller model

This simple model predicts completely specialized portfolios. For a given set of pre-tax returns on the dividend-paying stock (r_{div}) and the non-dividend paying stock (r_{nodiv}), the asset demand functions for the dividend stock (D_{div}) and for the non-dividend paying stock

(D_{nodiv}) for an investor with wealth level W are given by:

$$D_{div} = W, D_{nodiv} = 0 \text{ if } (1 - \tau_{div})r_{div} < r_{nodiv} \tag{1}$$

$$D_{div} = 0, D_{nodiv} = W \text{ if } (1 - \tau_{div})r_{div} > r_{nodiv} \tag{2}$$

Generalizing to the case of multiple equities with varying dividend yields, "high dividend paying stocks will be preferred by tax exempt organizations[1] and low income investors; those stocks yielding more of their return in the form of capital gains will gravitate to the taxpayers in the upper tax brackets" (Miller 1977).[2] This model also shows how clienteles can shift in response to changes in the tax rate structure. The tax rate that defines the cusp for household portfolio specialization in the simple model changes with the progressivity of the tax system. It is important to note that Miller's (1977) model concerns the equity market equilibrium and not an individual firm's choice over its payout policy. The model does not predict which firms pay dividends; indeed, from the perspective of any one firm, each clientele is as good as the next. That is, firms do not choose their dividend policy to attract a particular group of investors.

Miller's equilibrium provides intuition for how asset holding clienteles may emerge when investors face differences in tax rates. Yet the model is incomplete because it assumes all assets are riskless. When forming its equity portfolio, a household considers not only the impact of taxes on expected returns but also the riskiness of these holdings. To formally derive the relationship between tax rates and optimal dividend portfolio yields, I combine a model of optimal portfolio dividend yields, which defines the set of after-tax efficient portfolios for an investor with particular tax rates and risk preferences, with the after-tax

---

[1]There are additional non-tax reasons that tax-exempt institutional investors may form their own clientele. Because institutions are more likely to engage in "due diligence" and equilibrium prices make dividend-paying stocks more attractive to institutional investors, firms may use dividends to signal quality (Allen, Bernardo and Welch 2000).

[2]Where foreign investors align in the market for equities will depend on the tax treatment of his income derived from US equities in the US and in their country.

capital asset pricing model, which provides the equity market equilibrium conditions.

Characterizing an investor's portfolio maximization problem in terms of the mean and variance of portfolios, isoquants of after-tax returns are linear with slope $\frac{1-\tau_{cg}}{\tau_{div}-\tau_{cg}}$ and isoquants of portfolio variance are concentric ellipses in the expected return-dividend yield plane centered around the minimum-variance portfolio (Long 1977).[3] The locus of after-tax efficient portfolios are tangency points of these isoquants and are described by the following relationship between dividend yield and after-tax efficient portfolios:

$$\delta_p^i = b_0^i + b_1^i \bar{r}_p^i \tag{3}$$

where δ_p is the dividend yield of investor i's portfolio and $\bar{r}_p^i$ is investor i's expected return from portfolio p. The parameters b_0 and b_1 are individual-specific constants that are a function of the dividend and capital gains tax rates. The coefficient b_1 is inversely related to the tax rate variable, $\frac{\tau_{div}-\tau_{cg}}{1-\tau_{cg}}$, so the dividend yield of an after-tax efficient portfolio decreases with higher levels of expected returns. When the tax rate on dividends relative to capital gains taxes increases, b_1 rises. Thus for a given level of expected returns, portfolio dividend yields increase as their relative tax disadvantage falls. The household cannot do this without changing the level of portfolio risk, so Long's (1977) model does not give an unambiguous prediction about portfolio choices in response to a tax change.

To obtain such a market equilibrium condition, I combine Long's (1977) model of portfolio choice with the after-tax capital asset pricing model (Brennan (1970), Litzenberger and Ramaswamy (1979), Litzenberger and Ramaswamy (1980), Auerbach (1983), Auerbach and King (1983)), where the expected pre-tax return of stock j ($\bar{r}_j$) is a function of its pre-tax beta coefficient (β_j) and pre-tax dividend yield (δ_j):

$$\bar{r}_j = \gamma_0 + \gamma_1 \beta_j + \gamma_2 \delta_j \tag{4}$$

---

[3]Proof of this is provided in Appendix A of Long (1977).

That is, given two equities with the same risk exposure, the stock with a higher dividend yield must have a higher expected return to compensate for the tax burden associated with the dividend.

Substituting this condition into the investor demand equation yields the following relationship between pre-tax portfolio dividend yields and beta:

$$\delta_p^i = \frac{b_0^i + b_1^i \gamma_0 + b_1^i \gamma_1 \beta_p}{1 - b_1^i \gamma_2} \tag{5}$$

This equation implies a linear relationship between efficient portfolio dividend yields and portfolio risk, with the nature of this relationship (i.e., the slope and intercept of this line in dividend-risk space) determined by the relative dividend and capital gains tax rates. For a given level of risk, the compensation required for a higher dividend yield is positively related to the differential in tax rates on dividends and capital gains.[4]

3 Jobs and Growth Tax Relief Reconciliation Act of 2003

The Jobs and Growth Tax Relief Reconciliation Act of 2003 contained two major components relevant to this study. The first is reductions in long-term capital gains tax rates. The top capital gains marginal tax rate fell from 20% to 15%, while the 10% rate for lower-income individuals fell to 5% (and to zero percent in 2008). The second is that qualified dividends were now taxed at the same statutory rate as capital gains, rather than at the ordinary income marginal tax rate.[5] As a result, the top marginal tax rate for dividends fell from

---

[4]Without taxes, the "two-fund theorem" states that all investors hold some combination of riskless bonds and the market portfolio, where the proportion in each is determined by risk preference.

[5]Dividends from most foreign corporations, credit unions and banks were excluded from "qualified" dividend income. Non-qualified dividends remained taxed as part of ordinary income.

35% to 15%, and from 10% to 5% for lower income individuals.[6] This change was applied to dividends from directly held equities and those passed through by a mutual fund or other regulated investment company, partnership, REIT, or common trust fund.

Changes to statutory tax rates on capital gains and dividend income are depicted in Figure 2. Prior to the 2003 tax act, high-income individuals had a strong tax incentive to receive equity returns in the form of capital gains rather than dividends. Thus, portfolio dividend yields for high-income households are predicted to be lower than those for low-income households. The 2003 tax act completely closed the gap between dividend and capital gains tax rates, making dividend income more attractive for all households. That the change in the tax treatment was dramatic at high levels of income is also clear in Figure 2. Thus, portfolio dividend yields for higher-income households are predicted to grow by relatively more than those for lower-income households, *ceteris paribus*. It is this differentially dramatic decrease in the tax treatment of dividend income that is used to identify the effect of dividend and capital gains tax rates on household equity portfolio choices.

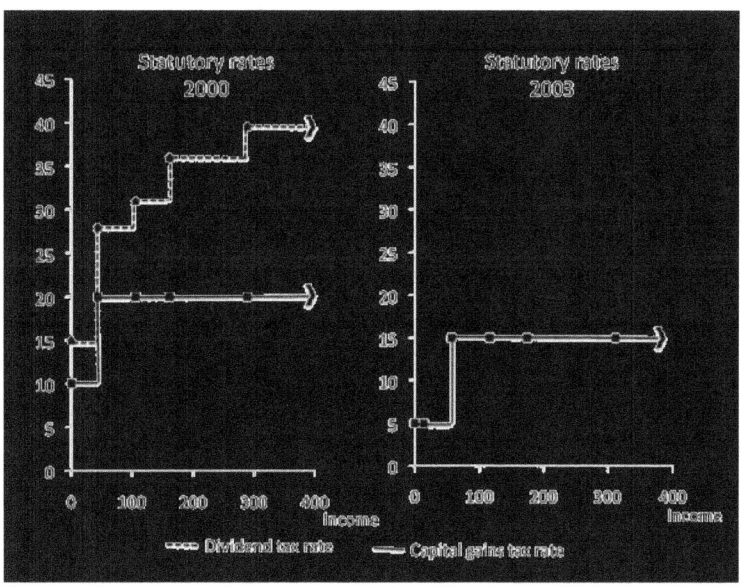

Figure 2: Statutory tax rates: Married couples filing jointly

---

[6]Taxpayers on the Alternative Minimum Tax schedule also benefited from the reduction by facing a reduction from the 28% flat rate to 15%.

4 Data and methodology

4.1 Description of data

In the main analysis, I use data from the 2001 and 2004 Surveys of Consumer Finances (SCF), a triennial survey conducted by the Federal Reserve Board of Governors that provides repeated cross-sectional data on wealth in the United States.[7] In analyzing the longer term household response to the 2003 tax act, I also use 2007 SCF data. The SCF contains detailed household-level information on assets and liabilities, which makes it one of the best data sources for studying household portfolios. The data additionally contain rich information on demographic characteristics and attitudes towards risk and credit.

The SCF includes 4,442 households in the 2001 sample, 4,519 in the 2004 sample and 4,418 in the 2007 sample. The sampling methodology of the SCF has two parts to improve coverage of U.S. households. One sample frame is from an area probability weighted sample derived from the Census Bureau's national sampling frame. The second frame is derived from the IRS Statistics of Income Individual Taxpayer File and is used to oversample high-income households. The oversampling of these households is important for identifying clientele effects since financial asset holdings are concentrated at the top end of the income distribution. Indeed, according to the 2001 SCF, 60.6% of families in the top 10th percentile of the income distribution held stocks, while only 3.5% of families in the bottom 20th percentile held stocks. In 2004, the percentages are 55.0% and 5.1%, respectively (Bucks, Kennickell and Moore 2006). Sampling weights are provided so estimates can be weighted to represent the U.S. household population in each year. The weighted sample represents 106.5, 112.1 and 116.1 million households in the 2001, 2004 and 2007 samples, respectively. All summary statistics and regressions presented in this paper are weighted using the sampling weights. Missing

---

[7]Panel data would allow me to observe household-specific changes in portfolios in response to the tax reform. While the SCF contains a panel component for the 1983 - 1989 waves, it does not for the period considered. That the SCF is repeated cross-sectional data rather than panel data does not change the interpretation of the parameter estimates (Heckman and Robb 1985).

values are replaced using a multiple imputation technique. These multiple imputations improve the efficiency of the point estimates by increasing the sample size, but as with any imputed values, require that the missing observations be conditionally random. All summary statistics, regressions and their standard errors are corrected for multiple imputations.[8]

The dependent variable is a household's portfolio dividend yield, defined as the ratio of the dollar value of dividend income to the dollar value of taxable equity. This measure represents a household's weighted-average dividend yield on its taxable equity. Dividend income is the dollar amount of ordinary dividend income received from stocks in taxable accounts in the previous calendar year.[9] Taxable equity is the sum of stocks held directly, stocks held through mutual funds, and stocks held in trusts, annuities, or other managed investment accounts. Equity held in mutual funds is the sum of the full value of stock mutual funds and half the value of combination mutual funds. The full value of other managed assets is included if it is mostly invested in stock, half the value if it is split between stocks and bonds, or stocks and money market accounts, and a third of the value if it is split between stocks, bonds, and money market accounts. The dollar value of equity is the market value at the time of interview, conducted in the second half of the survey year.[10] Stocks held in 401Ks, IRAs or other qualifying retirement accounts, as well as dividend income received from such securities, are not included in this measure. This exclusion is important because the tax rate reductions for dividends do not apply to equities in tax-deferred accounts. However, I am unable to identify if 2004 dividend yields contain stocks shifted between taxable and tax-deferred accounts. All components are adjusted to 2004 dollars.

---

[8]See Kennickell (1998) for an overview of the multiple imputation methodology.

[9]This value should correspond to item 9 on IRS form 1040 in 2000 and item 9a on IRS form 1040 in 2003/2006, and reported on a 1099-DIV.

[10]The 2001 SCF was conducted between May and December 2001, while the 2004 SCF was conducted between June 2004 and February 2005. The difference in timing may bias the yield measure if the equity holdings at the time of the survey are not representative of the equity holdings from which the dividend income was drawn. Unfortunately, there is no information in the survey that informs on the direction of this bias. Small denominator values may create outliers, so sensitivity checks to the influence of outliers are provided in the analysis.

To compute marginal tax rates on dividends and capital gains, I construct household adjusted gross income and deductions information from variables provided in the SCF. Then, I pass a flat file of these variables through the National Bureau of Economic Research's TAXSIM web program to compute statutory federal marginal tax rates.[11] The *effective* tax rate on long-term capital gains is lower than the statutory rate because taxes on capital gains are deferred until they are realized and because capital gains that are accrued until death qualify for a "basis step-up," which excuses the tax liability on such gains. I compute effective long term capital gains tax rates following (King and Fullerton 1984), who argue that the statutory tax rate on capital gains should be halved to account for the option value of tax-deferral, and halved again to account for the step-up basis at death and the selected realization of losses.[12]

Figure 3 is a plot of the average effective dividend and capital gains tax rate by income percentile computed from the two samples. This figure shows that the treatment effect is larger for high income households than for lower income households. Because the dividend clientele hypothesis regards the relative tax treatment of dividend income and capital gains, I use the difference in effective dividend and capital gains marginal tax rates as the main regressor of interest.[13] The gap between the two lines represents the absolute tax disadvantage of dividends.

The validity of using estimates from the SCF surveys to infer the effect of the 2003 tax

---

[11]Stata programs that convert SCF data into variables required for TAXSIM are available at the NBER website. The TAXSIM programs are found at http://www.nber.org/~taxsim/to-taxsim/. See Feenberg and Coutts (1993) for a description. State tax rates are a potentially useful source of tax rate variation. However, to maintain anonymity, state identifiers are omitted from the public SCF datasets so this information cannot be used.

[12]Ivkovic, Poterba and Weisbenner (2005) use individual stock holding data to estimate the effective capital gains tax rates for various stock holding patterns, prospective appreciation rates, and whether stocks were held in taxable or non-taxable accounts. Various assumptions provide a wide range of simulated effective tax rates. They do not have demographic information that might predict effective tax rates, so I use the long-established convention of using 25% of the statutory rate to measure the effective capital gains rate.

[13]This is the numerator of the tax rate variable described in equation 3. I use this measure because it nicely captures the relative tax disadvantage of dividends. This is the same tax variable used in Scholz (1992).

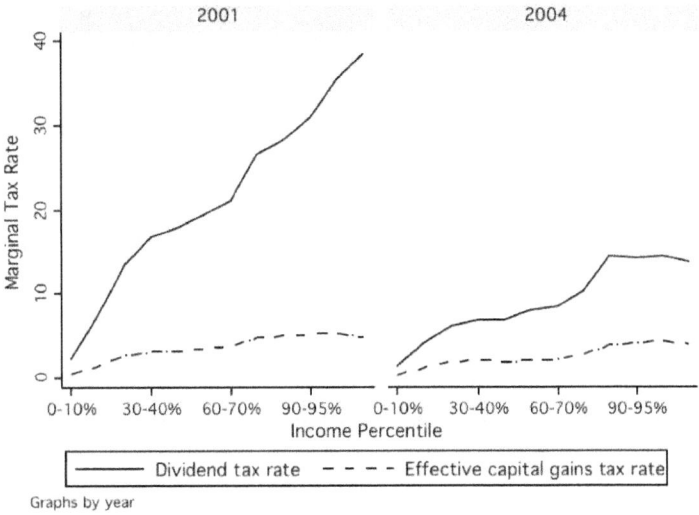

Figure 3: Empirical tax rate distribution

act depends in part on the timing of the tax changes and the surveys. Auerbach and Hassett (2007) document the key events leading to the 2003 tax act. Reductions in dividend tax rates were not seriously discussed prior to December 2002, suggesting that there was no anticipation of such a tax change before that time.[14] Notably, capital income tax rate cuts were not part of the 2000 Bush campaign platform. Since dividend income reported in the 2001 SCF sample are derived from equity holdings in 2000, these data are not impacted by the 2003 tax act. By the beginning of 2003, however, households and corporations knew that there was a significant probability that dividends would face a lower tax rate and that when a tax act was passed, the tax cuts would be applied retroactively to the beginning of 2003. The 2004 SCF contains information on dividend receipts from 2003, which are clearly impacted by the 2003 tax act. When the 2003 tax act was first passed, the reduced tax rates were set to expire in 2008. However, the Tax Increase Prevention and Reconciliation Act of

---

[14]The first notable mention of the reductions in the press occurred on December 25, 2002, when the Wall Street Journal reported that the Bush administration planned to reduce dividend tax rates by 50 percent. On January 6, 2003, the Wall Street Journal announced the Bush administration's plans to eliminate dividend taxes. Reductions to capital gains and dividend tax rates were officially proposed on January 7, 2003 by the Bush administration. The Conference Committee version of the 2003 tax act passed the House and Senate on May 23, 2003, and was signed into law on June 20, 2003.

2005 extended the reduced tax rates on dividends and capital gains through 2010.

A number of demographic characteristics are used to control for non-tax factors in the regression analysis that may influence household choices over portfolio dividend yields. Age categories, an indicator variable for being retired, and educational attainment categories are constructed to correspond to the head of household. Net worth categories and household size are computed for the household unit. Responses to a question about the "amount of financial risk that you or your (spouse/partner) [are] willing to take when you save money or make decisions" are used to construct proxies for risk preference. The risk-aversion indicator variable is set to one if respondents answered that they were "not willing to take financial risks," and zero otherwise. The "'moderate risk", "high risk" and "very high risk" indicator variables equal one if the respondent answered that they were willing to "take average financial risks expecting to earn average returns", "take above average financial risks expecting to earn above average returns", and "take substantial financial risks expecting to earn substantial returns" respectively, and zero otherwise. Summary statistics of these variables are presented in Table 1.

SCF data are self-reported, so measurement error may be of concern, particularly for sensitive data items such as components of wealth. Measurement error may arise when individuals have to sum up values over several financial accounts or because people are unwilling to accurately report such items. As an overall check of the dividends data, I compare dividend income reported in the SCF with that reported on tax returns provided by the IRS Statistics of Income (SOI) Tax Statistics publications. Unweighted, the dividend income reported in the SCF account for approximately 1% of dividend income reported on tax returns. In the SOI data, 26.3% and 23.3% of tax filers report that they received dividend income in 2000 and 2003, respectively. Of the SCF households, only 16.8% and 15.5% report positive dividend income in the 2001 and 2004 surveys, respectively. This difference could reflect that some households with relatively little dividend income do not remember such

Table 1: Summary statistics of demographic and socioeconomic variables

Variable	2001	2004	2007
Share of SCF Sample			
Income (thousands)			
0-15	0.14	0.14	0.13
15-25	0.11	0.12	0.13
25-50	0.27	0.26	0.27
50-75	0.16	0.18	0.17
75-100	0.12	0.10	0.11
100-250	0.15	0.17	0.16
250+	0.03	0.03	0.04
Net worth (thousands)			
0-50	0.38	0.38	0.36
50-100	0.12	0.11	0.10
100-250	0.19	0.18	0.19
250-1000	0.23	0.23	0.25
1000+	0.09	0.09	0.09
Demographic characteristics			
No degree	0.09	0.09	0.09
High school degree	0.31	0.30	0.32
Some college but no college degree	0.18	0.18	0.18
College degree	0.34	0.37	0.35
Not willing to take financial risks	0.40	0.42	0.42
Female	0.27	0.28	0.28
Married	0.60	0.58	0.59
Household size	2.41	2.39	2.42
Retired	0.19	0.19	0.19
Average Age	48.97	49.56	50.01
Number of households (millions)	106.5	112.1	116.1
Number of observations	4519	4442	4418

Observations are weighted by their sampling weights. Financial data
are in 2004 dollars. Demographic characteristics refer to the head
of household. Statistics are corrected for multiple imputations.

income or think it is not important enough to report. In the SOI, individuals report $142 and $111 billion in dividend income in 2000 and 2003, respectively, whereas the SCF accounts for $108 and $107 billion in the 2001 and 2004 surveys, respectively. In the aggregate, the SOI and SCF data provide information that is fairly consistent, though substantial measurement error at the individual level may remain.[15] In the remaining analysis, I implicitly assume that measurement error is time invariant conditional on treatment group, which allows the main estimates to remain consistent.

Before turning to the empirical models, I report on some patterns in dividend yields in the data. Interestingly, many equity-holding households report that they receive zero income from dividends. In fact, 55.7% and 57.4% of equity-holding households are computed to have a zero dividend yield in 2001 and 2004, respectively.[16] Thus, when considering portfolio dividend yields, there will be a mass point at zero. The proportion of equities held and dividends received by income percentiles is presented in Table 2. The percentage of dividends received by households in the top 5% increased substantially between the 2001 and 2004 surveys while the percentage of equities remained roughly the same. This provides evidence that denominator effects are not driving the regression results to follow. Regardless, dividend clientele effects are about the ratio of dividend income to equity holdings, so predictions about dividend clienteles remain the same even if equity valuations changed. Table 2 also presents information about the percentage of income that was received from dividends from the SCF samples. This provides casual evidence that the highest income households increased their dividend income by relatively more than lower-income households.

---

[15]Antoniewicz (1996) compares the SCF with the Federal Reserve's Flow of Funds (FOF) data, which are based off reports by financial institutions, and finds that the two are fairly consistent after adjusting for differences in variable definitions.

[16]Information on publicly traded stocks from CRSP reveals that between 75% to 80% of publicly traded stocks do not pay dividends.

Table 2: Dividend receipts and equity holdings by income

Income Percentile	Percentage of total dividends			Percentage of total equity			Dividends as a percent of income		
	2001	2004	2007	2001	2004	2007	2001	2004	2007
0-10	1.21	0.98	0.84	0.80	0.97	1.49	1.42	0.90	0.47
10-20	0.57	0.35	0.60	0.60	0.41	0.64	0.43	0.28	0.54
20-30	1.57	1.20	1.19	0.90	1.01	1.04	0.74	0.46	0.63
30-40	2.30	0.88	0.93	2.28	1.84	2.70	0.70	0.28	0.30
40-50	3.31	1.15	1.87	1.85	2.23	1.45	0.97	0.28	0.60
50-60	5.18	3.30	1.29	3.48	3.93	1.80	1.13	0.70	0.31
60-70	6.13	4.93	4.58	5.82	5.98	4.30	0.96	0.73	0.94
70-80	4.33	4.23	6.34	6.34	5.99	7.57	0.53	0.50	0.92
80-90	10.54	6.45	8.60	9.86	7.96	7.12	1.04	0.59	0.91
90-95	13.39	7.36	5.44	10.89	8.61	6.89	1.88	0.88	0.84
95-99	23.59	26.64	24.92	28.58	24.69	25.14	2.09	2.15	2.14
99-100	27.88	42.53	43.39	28.59	36.39	39.86	2.03	3.32	3.08

Source: Author's calculations using SCF data. Observations are weighted by their SCF sampling weights. Statistics are corrected for multiple imputations.

4.2 Estimation strategy

To examine the existence of tax-based dividend clienteles, I consider the relationship between household portfolio dividend yields and tax rates. Because I am interested in the mix of equities that households choose to hold, rather than the choice of whether to hold equities, I focus on equity-holding households in the main analysis. Additionally, I exclude 7 observations with dividend yields of over 1000%.[17] I use several other cut-off values in the sensitivity analysis to ensure that the main estimates are robust to this choice. Since many equity-holding households do not receive dividend income, there is a mass point in the dependent variable at zero. I treat these observations with dividend yields equal to zero as households for whom no dividend income is preferred to receiving some. This suggests a censored regression model (Type II Tobit) that Wooldridge (2002) calls the "corner solution model" because there is a mass point that results from household optimization.

---

[17]These large outliers likely arise because some households who received dividend income in the year prior to the survey liquidated their equity holdings by the time of the survey. When excluding households with yields over 1000%, the maximum dividend yield is 650%.

The estimating equation for the treatment effects model of the effect of taxes on portfolio dividend yields that incorporates the Tobit framework is given by:

$$Y_{it}^* = X_{it}\beta + \alpha\tau_t(x_{it}) + \varepsilon_{it}$$

$$Y_{it} = \max\{0, X_{it}\beta + \alpha\tau_t(x_{it}) + \varepsilon_{it}\} \tag{6}$$

where Y^* is the latent (uncensored) dividend yield, Y is the observed (censored) dividend yield, i corresponds to the household and t denotes the time period. The vector X contains factors other than taxes that may affect household choices over dividend yields. The continuous treatment variable is $\tau_t(x_{it})$, the difference in dividend and capital gains marginal tax rates. It is a function of various household characteristics, such as income, marital status, and family structure. The vector x contains a subset of X. Note that the tax function is indexed only by t because all households face the same tax schedule at a given point in time. That is, two households with the same values of x_{it} face the same tax rates.

The parameter of interest is a function of α, the effect of the tax treatment on portfolio dividend yields. Specifically, because this is a corner solution model the marginal effect of interest is that on the observed dividend yield. In principle, α could be identified from a single cross-section of data because it enters the equation linearly and the tax schedule is nonlinear (Scholz 1992). Such identification is weak, however, and thus undesirable in practice. Because all households face the same tax system at a given point in time, two households with the same level of income will face different tax rates only through differences in other characteristics. When variations in economic situations, such as income levels and family structure, are the driving source of variation in marginal tax rates that a household faces, it is difficult to disentangle income effects (and other factors that are correlated with income) from pure tax effects in a single cross-section. Identification of the tax effect is achieved only through the nonlinearities in the tax schedule, which is typically weak in

18

practice. For example, if income impacts dividend yields nonlinearly but we only include the level of income in the regression, then the nonlinearity in the tax schedule used to identify the tax effect is partly due to the nonlinearity of the income effect, and so would confound income effects and tax effects.

Instead, the 2003 tax act provides exogenous variation in tax rates that can be used to identify α. Because the SCF is a repeated cross-section rather than a panel, we cannot follow the same individuals over time. Assuming that the two cross-sections are independent, which likely holds given the sampling design of the survey, we can pool the data across the periods and estimate α:

$$Y_{i,s}^* = \alpha[\tau_{2003}(x_{i,2004}) - \tau_{2000}(x_{i,2001})]\mathbb{I}(SCF = 2004) + \alpha\tau_{2000}(x_{i,2001})$$

$$+ \eta\mathbb{I}(SCF = 2004) + X_{i,s}\beta + \varepsilon_{i,s}$$

$$Y_{i,s} = \max\{0, Y_{i,s}^*\}, \quad s \in (2001, 2004) \tag{7}$$

where $\mathbb{I}(SCF = 2004)$ is an indicator variable that equals one if the observation is from the 2004 SCF and zero if the observation is from the 2001 SCF. Note that the year subscripts for the tax function, τ, and its inputs, x, differ by one year to reflect that the survey data contains income information for the previous calendar year. Conditional on the observed variables, α is identified from people with the same vector of X characteristics facing two different sets of tax rates because of the 2003 tax act.

The post-treatment indicator variable, $\mathbb{I}(SCF = 2004)$, controls for the average difference in portfolio dividend yields across SCF samples. This is important because there is a well-documented increase in the supply of dividends following the 2003 tax act (Chetty and Saez (2005), Brown et al. (2004)). Perhaps most notably, Microsoft initiated a dividend payment for the first time immediately following the 2003 tax act. Such changes in dividend policies affect market prices, so dividend yields are expected to change between the two samples.

19

That firms altered dividend policies and market prices changed in response does not affect the interpretation of the tax effect. This is because the dividend clientele hypothesis regards differences in portfolio dividend yields across investors. It does not matter if the response to the 2003 tax act comes through changes in the numerator or denominator of the dividend yield measure since either reflects the types of equities that a household chooses to hold.

Because households can affect their tax rates through their portfolio dividend yield choices, the actual difference in marginal tax rates on dividends and capital gains is endogenous. To solve this endogeneity problem, I use instrumental variable techniques to consistently estimate α. Moffitt and Wilhelm (2000) show that when a tax reform changes tax rates by different intensities across groups, a valid grouping variable for a difference-in-differences analysis can instrument for the change in tax rates. The 2003 tax act provides both a natural experiment and a grouping variable. Educational attainment is correlated with permanent income, and thus marginal tax rates (Eissa (1996b), Blundell, Duncan and Meghir (1998), Moffitt and Wilhelm (2000)).[18] Because it is unlikely that households manipulated their choice of education in response to the 2003 tax act, particularly in such a short time frame, educational attainment is uncorrelated with transitory income and with behavioral responses to the tax change. I use an indicator for whether the household head has a college degree as the difference-in-differences grouping variable.[19] Thus, one of the key identifying assumptions is that non-tax factors that influence dividend yield choices did not change differentially by treatment group across the 2003 tax act.

The estimated model is Amemiya's generalized least squares estimator for a limited dependent variable with endogenous regressors (Amemiya (1978), Amemiya (1979)), described by the following system:

---

[18]For an example of how difference-in-differences has been used to examine the impact of a tax policy, see Eissa (1996a) and Heckman's (1996) response to Eissa (1996a).

[19]If this endogeneity is ignored, the estimated tax effect will be biased upwards (towards zero) because households may reduce their dividend income to reduce their tax liability. Indeed, when I use actual marginal tax rates in the main regressions, the estimated tax effect is closer to zero (and sometimes even positive), though no longer statistically significant.

$$Y_{i,s}^* = \alpha[\tau_{2003}(x_{i,2004}) - \tau_{2000}(x_{i,2001})]\mathbb{I}(SCF = 2004) + \alpha\tau_{2000}(x_{i,2001})$$

$$+ \eta\mathbb{I}(SCF = 2004) + X_{i,s}\beta + \varepsilon_{i,s}$$

$$Y_{i,s} = \max\{0, Y_{i,s}^*\}, \quad s \in (2001, 2004)$$

$$\tau_s(x_{i,s}) = \gamma_0 + \gamma_1\{college * \mathbb{I}(SCF = 2004)\}_{i,s} + \gamma_2\mathbb{I}(SCF = 2004)_{i,s} + X_{i,s}\xi + u_{i,s} \quad (8)$$

where *college* is an indicator variable that equals one if the head-of-household has at least a college degree, and zero otherwise. The interaction term $college*\mathbb{I}(SCF = 2004)$ instruments for receiving the high tax treatment of the 2003 tax act. Note that *college* is included in the vector X and proxies for the average difference in financial sophistication across treatment groups. The model is estimated by maximum likelihood where the estimating equation is equation 5.6 in Newey (1987).

The variables included in X are used to control for other non-tax factors that may affect household portfolio dividend yields. This is important because the composition of households in each group may differ over time. Including these characteristics also improves the efficiency of treatment effect estimates by reducing the residual variance of the regression. First, life-cycle models predict that older individuals and those with a greater need for a steady income flow will prefer steady dividend payments to finance consumption (Shefrin and Thaler 1988). To account for such preferences, I include age categories, an indicator variable for whether the household head is retired, and household size (level and square).[20] Transaction costs associated with liquidating stock to realize capital gains may cause individuals to prefer the consistency of dividend payments (Leape 1987). Because the importance of transaction costs

---

[20]Shefrin and Statman (1984) argue that some investors maintain separate "mental accounts" for dividend income and capital gains because of self-control problems or regret aversion. This effect cannot be identified in SCF data. Theories of why firms pay dividends may also be informative. If dividends alleviate agency problems between firms and investors (Jensen and Meckling 1976) or signal the future profitability of a firm (Bhattacharya (1979), Bernheim (1991)), investors with high marginal tax rates may prefer high dividend-yield securities despite their tax disadvantage.

is likely a function of the size of such costs relative to overall wealth, I include net worth groups in the estimation. In addition, information costs associated with acquiring an asset may be important for portfolio choices. Educational attainment measures are used to proxy for the importance of information costs and financial sophistication. Lastly, risk-averse households may prefer to receive payments in the relatively consistent form of dividends, rather than be subject to price fluctuations in capital markets. Risk preference proxies derived from self-reports of the household's willingness to participate in financial markets are used.

Figure 4 presents average portfolio dividend yields by education group and year, weighted by both SCF sampling weights and the value of equity holdings. Weighting by equity valuations dampens the influence of outliers caused by small equity holdings. This figure provides suggestive evidence for the dividend clientele hypothesis. In the 2001 sample, when dividends are very tax disadvantaged for high income individuals, the no college group has a higher dividend yield than the college-educated group. This is consistent with the sorting predicted by the dividend clientele hypothesis. The 2003 tax act reduced the relative tax disadvantage of dividends for all individuals, but especially for high-income households. In the 2004 data, the dividend yield pattern is reversed so that college-educated households increased their dividend yields by more than households without a college degree. In the aggregate, the group average yields are supportive of the dividend clientele hypothesis.

As a basic check of the validity of using educational attainment measures as a grouping variable, Table 3 provides summary statistics for households by education class and year. The difference in tax treatment intensities is preserved by the grouping variable, suggesting that the instrument is relevant for the endogenous tax rate variable. Table 3 also provides the p-value for a test that a characteristic evolves differentially across groups. This is the

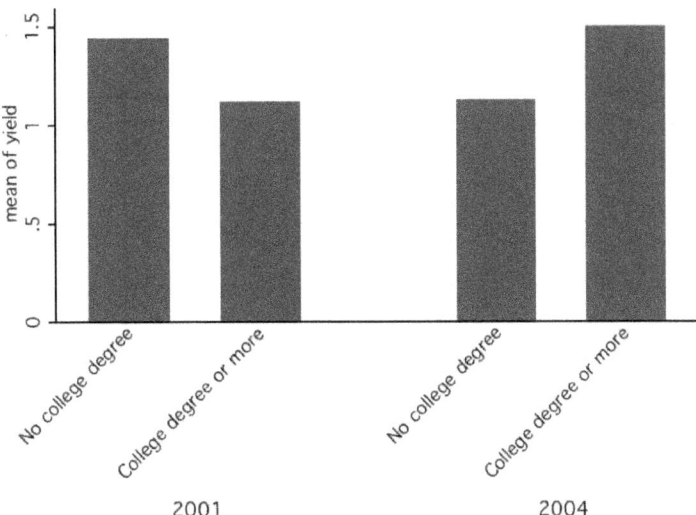

Figure 4: Portfolio dividend yields by educational attainment, 2001 and 2004

p-value on β_2 in the following difference-in-differences regression:

$$characteristic_{i,t} = \beta_0 + \beta_1 college_{i,t} + \beta_2 college * \mathbb{I}(SCF = 2004)_{i,t} + u_{it} \qquad (9)$$

Importantly, these characteristics are not changing differentially across groups in the two samples. The statistically different change in tax rates does not appear to be due to differential changes in income. Additionally, the proportion of households in each group is stable, so considering the sample of equity-holding households in each education class also appears to be appropriate.

Because this analysis focuses on equity-holding households, the assumption that the composition of groups is stable across periods may be violated. Indeed, several studies find that taxes influence stock ownership probabilities (Poterba and Samwick (2002), King and Leape (1998). To test whether the 2003 tax act altered the population of equity-holders, I estimate a difference-in-differences probit for the probability of holding equities. Table 4 presents results from this estimation. The parameters of interest, the coefficients for $college * y04$ and $y04$, are not statistically significant and I fail to reject the null hypothesis

23

Table 3: Characteristics of equity-holders, medians by education group

| | No college degree | | College degree | | p-value on |
	2001	2004	2001	2004	diff-in-diff
Tax differential	15.8	7.1	22.3	10.0	0.00
Income (thousands, median)	58.9	60.0	103.4	104.3	0.34
Percent with dividend income	34.9	32.3	51.2	49.4	0.85
Not willing to take financial risk	20.1	22.9	8.1	8.6	0.49
Percent married	68.0	63.8	75.3	72.3	0.83
Percent retired	25.3	28.7	16.0	16.9	0.57
Age	51.4	54.6	49.8	51.0	0.23
Household size	2.3	2.3	2.6	2.5	0.47
Number of observations	608	533	1387	1429	

Each observations is weighted by its SCF sampling weight. Statistics are corrected for multiple imputations. Demographic characteristics correspond to the head of household. The p-value for test for differences in income corresponds to a test of differences in mean income.

that equity-holding households did not change across the two periods. Thus, changes in dividend yields across treatment groups are not likely to be due to the 2003 tax act causing new households to enter equity markets.

The validity of a difference-in-differences approach relies on the assumption that the growth rate of the dependent variable would be equal across groups in the absence of treatment. Otherwise, the estimated treatment effect may partly reflect other differences across groups. Figure 5 presents household portfolio dividend yields by education groups from the 1992, 1995, 1998 and 2001 SCF samples. The trends in dividend yields look quite similar between the two groups.[21] To test this more formally, I run a regression of portfolio dividend yields on a linear trend, a dummy variable for whether or not the head of household has a college degree, and the interaction of the college indicator variable and the linear trend:

$$yield = \beta_0 + \beta_1 trend + \beta_2 college + \beta_3 college * trend + \varepsilon. \tag{10}$$

---

[21] The decreasing trend in dividend yields is consistent with the well-documented reduction in firm dividend payments in favor of share repurchases as a means of distributing profits to their shareholders.

Table 4: Probit model for holding equities

Variable	Estimated Marginal Effect	Std. Error	p-value
College * y04	-0.01	0.02	0.58
College	0.11	0.02	0.00
SCF = 2004	-0.01	0.01	0.41
Retired	0.04	0.02	0.05
Married	0.05	0.02	0.00
Household size	-0.06	0.02	0.00
Household size (squared)	0.01	0.00	0.00
Net worth 50,000-100,000	0.10	0.02	0.00
Net worth 100,000-250,000	0.17	0.01	0.00
Net worth 250,000-1,000,000	0.31	0.01	0.00
Net worth >1,000,000	0.56	0.02	0.00
Not willing to take financial risk	-0.22	0.01	0.00

Presented estimates are average marginal effects. Standard errors are heteroskedasticity robust. Observations are weighted by their SCF sampling weights. Estimates are corrected for multiple imputations. Age categories are included but estimates are not reported. None are statistically significant. The full table of results is available upon request.

A test for the difference in slope coefficients for the two groups over time is equivalent to a test that the coefficient on the interaction term (β_3) is zero. In this regression, the p-value for the test that β_3 is zero is 0.98 and I fail to reject the null.[22]

While nonlinear instrumental variables models are not literally estimated in two stages, I run what would be the first stage regression in the linear case to ascertain the instruments' strength. Table 5 shows select results from this estimation. Because of the different intensities of the 2003 tax changes, we should expect that college-educated households experienced a larger decrease in the tax differential than those without a college education. Indeed, the parameter estimate on the treatment effects variable is negative and statistically significant. The F-statistic for the exclusion restriction is 28.45. Because the critical value of a 5% Wald

---

[22]When allowing for a quadratic trend differences in trends across the two groups remains statistically insignificant. The p-values on the linear and quadratic trend-interaction terms are 0.35 and 0.34, respectively.

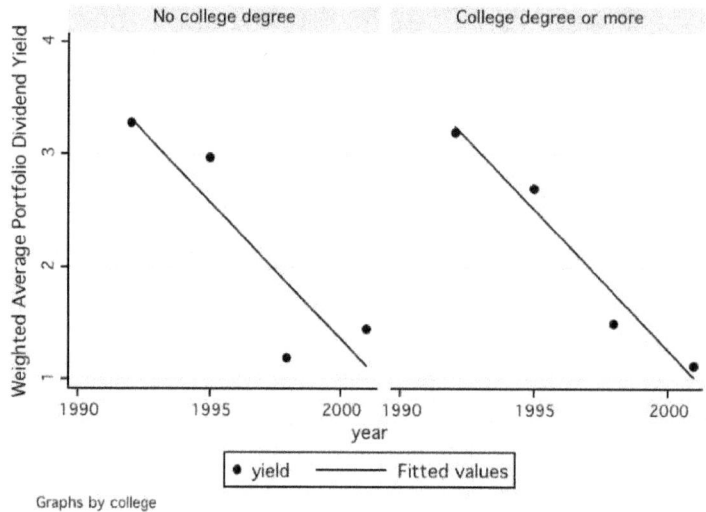

Figure 5: Trends in portfolio dividend yields by educational attainment group

test is 16.38,[23] the hypothesis that the high treatment indicator is a weak instrument is rejected. To test that using the instrumental variables techniques is necessary, I perform the test of exogeneity for the Tobit model proposed by Smith and Blundell (1986).[24] The null hypothesis that all the regressors are exogenous is rejected at the 5% level.

5 Results and discussion

5.1 Baseline results

Table 6 presents the average marginal effect of the covariates on observed dividend yields derived from the instrumental variables Tobit regression results.[25] According to the dividend clientele hypothesis, as dividends become more tax-disadvantaged relative to capital gains

---

[23]See Stock and Yogo (2002) for critical values for a test of weak instruments.

[24]This test expresses the suspected endogenous regressors as a linear projection of the instruments, and the residuals from that regression are added to the original model. If the model is correctly specified and the regressors are exogenous, the residuals from the first-stage should have no explanatory power in the second-stage regression.

[25]This is the appropriate marginal effect from the Tobit model because an observed zero dividend yield is the result of a choice rather than censoring. This marginal effect is computed as $\Phi(\frac{X\beta}{\sigma})\beta_j$. See Cameron and Trivedi (2006) pp. 541-542 for a derivation.

Table 5: "First-stage" regression results
Dependent variable: Dividend and capital gains tax rate differential

Variables	Est. Coeff.	Std. Error	p-value
College * 2004	-3.55	0.68	0.00
2004 SCF dummy	-8.58	0.55	0.00
College	4.14	0.65	0.00
Constant	12.30	1.14	0.00
Observations		3965	
R-squared		0.48	
F-statistic for instrument		28.45	
F-statistic for model		154.84	

All observations are weighted by their SCF sampling weight. Standard errors are heteroskedasticity-robust and are corrected for multiple imputations. Other controls are included in the regressions but not reported: age and net worth categories, household size (level and square), indicator variables for head being retired/married, and risk preference proxies.

(i.e., the dividend and capital gains tax rates differential, τ, becomes larger), households choose to hold equities with lower dividend yields. Indeed, the coefficient on the dividend and capital gains tax rate differential is negative and statistically significant at the 5% level.[26] To interpret the year effect, its magnitude must be calibrated against the average effect of the change in tax rates, 3.87. This is because one of the macroeconomic factors that changed between the two samples is the tax schedule. Thus, the average change to *observed* portfolio dividend yields across the two samples is very close to zero at -0.18 percentage points. To gauge the magnitude of this effect, note that the dividend yield on the S&P 500 index increased from 1.23% to 1.61% between 2000 and 2003.

That the effect of taxes on portfolio dividend yields is statistically significant does not inform upon the economic importance of the dividend clientele effect. To interpret the economic significance of the coefficient on the tax rate differential, first consider the impact

---

[26]Excluding the net worth categories, the parameter estimate on the tax rate differential effect is -0.33 (std. error = 0.16). Two survey questions ask how intensely households search for the best terms when making savings and investment decisions. When including proxy variables for "shopping intensity" constructed from these questions, the parameter estimate on the tax rate differential is roughly the same at -0.30 (std. error = 0.14) and the shopping variables are not significantly different from zero.

Table 6: Instrumental variable Tobit results
Dependent variable: Portfolio dividend yield
Instrumental variable: *College* ∗ *y*04 (High treatment indicator)

Variable	Estimated Marginal Effect Effect	Std. Error	p-value
Tax differential	-0.31	0.14	0.03
Age 25-35	3.94	1.81	0.03
Age 35-45	4.51	2.2	0.04
Age 45-55	5.42	2.69	0.04
Age 55-65	5.15	2.5	0.04
Over 65	4.92	2.29	0.03
Retired	-0.79	0.92	0.39
College	1.87	0.88	0.03
Net worth 50,000-100,000	-0.35	1.32	0.79
Net worth 100,000-250,000	0.05	1.23	0.97
Net worth 250,000-1,000,000	2.58	1.4	0.07
Net worth >1,000,000	5.06	2.18	0.02
Not willing to take financial risk	-1.79	1.12	0.11
Willing to take average financial risk	-0.34	0.6	0.57
Willing to take high financial risk	0.05	0.64	0.94
SCF = 2004	-4.05	1.74	0.02
Constant	-3.07	1.54	0.05
Number of observations		3956	
Number of uncensored observations		2379	

Marginal effects are effects on observed dividend yields. Standard errors are computed
using the Delta Method and are heteroskedasticity-robust. Observations are weighted
by their SCF sampling weights. Estimates are corrected for multiple imputations. Included
in the regressions but not reported are an indicator for the household head being married
and household size (level and square). None are statistically significant at the 5% level.

of the 2003 tax act on dividend yields of portfolios of households at different tax brackets,
summarized in Table 7. A household in the highest tax bracket would have faced a decrease
in the tax rate differential from 34.6 percentage points to 11.25 percentage points, leading
portfolio dividend yields to increase by 7.24 (=[11.25-34.6]*-0.31) percentage points. On
average, macroeconomic factors are estimated to decrease yields by 4.05 percentage points
(the estimate of η) for all households between 2001 and 2004. Thus, the predicted change
in observed portfolio dividend yields for households in the highest tax bracket is a 3.19

percentage point increase. Relative to an average portfolio yield for households in the top bracket in 2001 of 2.7 percentage points, this is a 115% increase in dividend yields. This constitutes a large and economically substantive response. Similar calculations are done for households in the next two tax brackets, which shows that the tax effect is large and varies substantially with the intensity of the tax treatment.[27]

Table 7: Effect of the 2003 tax act for select tax brackets

	Highest Bracket 39.6%	Next Bracket 36 %	Two below 31%
Tax rate differential, 2003	11.25	11.25	11.25
Tax rate differential, 2000	34.60	31.00	26.00
Change in tax rate differential	-23.35	-19.75	-14.75
Predicted change in yields $(\tau_{2003} - \tau_{2000}) * \hat{\beta}_\tau + \hat{\beta}_{y04}$	3.1	2.1	0.5
Average yield in 2001 sample	2.7	6.5	2.4
Percent change	115	32	21

Author's calculations based on the regression results in Table 6 and SCF data.

The previous exercise provides estimates of the impact of the 2003 tax act at particular points in the tax schedule. However, the realized economic impact of the 2003 tax act is better understood as the average portfolio response weighted by the proportion of households at various points of the income distribution. To obtain this estimate, I take households from the 2001 SCF sample and use TAXSIM to compute the tax rates that they would have faced under the 2003 tax rules. This change between a household's actual tax rates in 2000 and its simulated tax rates for 2003 is exogenous to household decisions in response to the 2003 tax act. I use these simulated tax rate changes and the estimated effect of the dividend and capital gains tax rate differential on portfolio dividend yields to compute the household-specific predicted change in dividend yields caused by the 2003 tax act.

Based on these simulations, college-educated households increased their portfolio div-

---

[27]The parameter estimates are interpreted as the effect of small changes in tax rates. With large changes to tax rates, these simulated responses are only approximations and unmodeled nonlinearities in the response function could make this estimate inaccurate. However, given the nature of the data, this is still the best way to understand the magnitude of the tax effect.

idend yields by 4.26 percentage points with an average yield in 2001 of 1.22% (standard deviation of 2.5%), whereas non-college educated households increased their portfolio dividend yields by 3.32 percentage points with an average yield of 2.23% in 2001 (standard deviation of 8.53%).[28] Thus, the treatment effect of the 2003 tax act is a 0.94 percentage point differential response in portfolio dividend yields between educational attainment groups. This estimated effect of the 2003 tax act is both economically significant and of plausible magnitude. Figure 6 depicts the actual portfolio dividend yields in 2001 and 2004, along with the predicted dividend yields in 2004 based on these simulations. As before, the predicted dividend yields are the predicted yields scaled by the year fixed effect. The predicted yields broadly match the patterns that are observed in 2004.

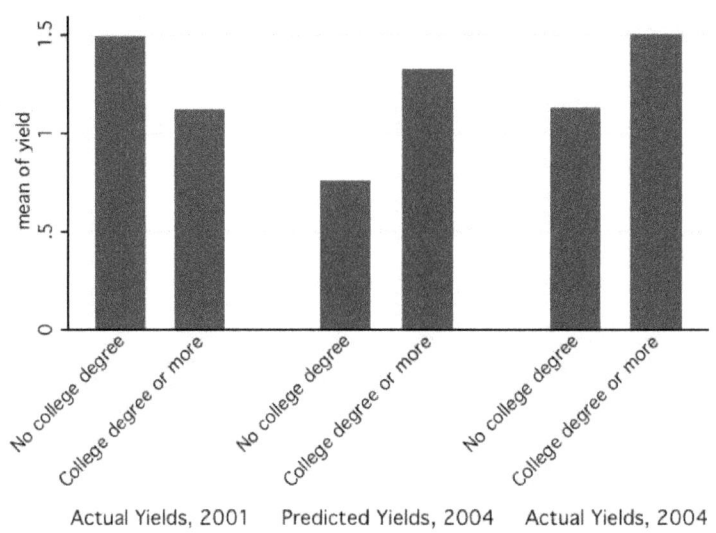

Figure 6: Comparing simulated change in portfolio dividend yields with actual yields

The estimated tax effect is a general equilibrium response that captures both changes to investor demands and changes to the supply of dividends. Because the SCF data is a repeated cross-section and does not contain information on the stocks in a household's

---

[28]This calculation is $\frac{1}{N}\sum_{i=1}^{N}(\hat{\tau}_i^{2003} - \tau_i^{2000})\hat{\beta}_\tau$, where $\hat{\tau}_i^{2003}$ is the tax rate differential that household i would have faced under the 2003 tax rules, τ_i^{2000} is the tax rate differential for household i in 2000, and $\hat{\beta}_\tau$ is the estimated marginal effect of the tax rate differential on portfolio dividend yields. This is computed for all equity-holding households in the 2001 SCF.

portfolio, active portfolio rebalancing (i.e., the sale and purchase of stocks) and passive rebalancing (i.e., the equities a household held before the tax act changed payout policies) are empirically indistinguishable. While the mechanism through which portfolio adjustments occur is interesting, it does not affect the interpretation of the tax effect. If portfolio adjustments are costless, households instantaneously adjust their portfolios in response to changes to firm dividend payout policies. In this case, household portfolios in the 2004 SCF reflect optimal portfolios after the 2003 tax act. At the other extreme with infinite adjustment costs, changes to household portfolio yields only reflect changes to firm policies. In this case, the estimated tax effect implies that households sorted according to the dividend clientele hypothesis prior to the tax act and firm responses were targeted at investors who would benefit the most.[29]

The nature of portfolio adjustments likely falls between these two extremes. Indeed, there is evidence for both active and passive portfolio adjustments. Lightner, Morrow, Ricketts and Riley (2008) find that abnormal returns following key events leading to the passage of the 2003 tax act are positively related to an equity's dividend yield. They interpret this result as evidence of active portfolio shifting. In addition, several investment companies began offering "high dividend yield" mutual funds in 2003, which indicates that there was an ability to increase portfolio dividend yields even through the selection of mutual funds. Chetty and Saez (2005) find that dividend initiations and increases following the 2003 tax act occurred among those firms whose equities were largely held by taxable investors, suggesting that firms were influenced by institutional investor preferences. Thus, the change in household portfolios in response to the 2003 tax act likely contains both active and passive portfolio adjustments.

With transaction costs, lags in portfolio adjustments may bias the longer term treatment

---

[29]See Hamada and Scholes (1985) for a discussion of how the tax characteristics of a firm's investors may influence the firm's optimal payout policy. However, the Brav, Graham, Harvey and Michaely (2005) survey of financial executives indicates that managers consider the tax preferences of their investors to be of secondary importance, at best, when making decisions over payout policies.

effect in either direction. The direction of the bias depends on how the household would adjust their portfolios barring transaction constraints, i.e., towards stocks with higher or lower dividend yields. In addition, there may be differences in adjustment periods across households that are important for understanding the effect of the 2003 tax act. If high-income households adjust their portfolios faster than lower income households, then the estimated treatment effect parameter overstates the long term relative responsiveness of affluent households to taxes. This may happen if high-income households respond faster because they face stronger financial incentive to adjust their portfolios. These households may also be more aware of tax code changes and their implications for optimal portfolio choices.[30] However, these parameter estimates are unbiased estimates of the average treatment effect by the time of data collection.[31]

Aside from tax effects, other parameter estimates are interesting to note. Life-cycle models of clientele formation are supported by the data. The age coefficients are all positive and statistically significant, and importantly are increasing in age. This is consistent with the hypothesis that older individuals prefer a steady stream of payments to finance their consumption. The estimated age effect could in part reflect a cohort effect. For example, those born before 1939 (i.e., those who are 65 years or older at the time of the 2004 survey) may prefer steadier flows of income from dividends because of experiences during the Depression.

High educational attainment and high net worth have a positive and significant effect on dividend yields. This relationship is consistent with signaling models in which firms pay dividends to attract more sophisticated investors. To the extent that education and investment sophistication are correlated, these results are consistent with empirical evidence that unsophisticated investors trade too frequently. Risk measures do not statistically significantly

---

[30]Kezdi and Willis (2003) argue that a lack of financial literacy may cause households to choose suboptimal portfolios. Financial literacy may affect other aspects of portfolio choice, such as adjusting to changes in tax policy.

[31]Date of interview information could be leveraged to examine if portfolio adjustments were lagged and to test whether those with a college degree responded more quickly than those who did not. The date of interview is not contained in the public version of the Survey of Consumer Finances, however.

influence portfolio dividend yields. Risk preferences might matter more for a household's allocation of wealth between debt and equity, rather than the types of equity that it chooses to hold. Also, self-reported measures of risk preferences may not accurately reflect cross-sectional differences across households.

Because older households may be more financially sophisticated due to prolonged experience with financial markets, older college-educated households may respond more quickly to tax policy changes than others. To account for this possibility, I run the same instrumental variables Tobit specification including interaction terms between the age categories and retired indicator variable with the treatment group indicator. In this specification, parameter estimates on the interaction terms are not statistically significantly different from zero and the estimated tax rate differential effect remains roughly the same. The effects of these controls on portfolio dividend yields do not appear to change over the two periods considered.

In addition, optimism over the future state of the economy has been shown to influence portfolio choices, particularly the decision of whether to hold stocks (Kezdi and Willis 2003). If investors believe that dividends signal safety, then optimistic households may choose lower dividend yields, *ceteris paribus*. Responses to the question, "Over the next five years, do you expect the U.S. economy as a whole to perform better, worse, or about the same as it has over the past five years?" are used to construct indicator variables for households who believe the economy will perform better, worse and about the same. When including this measure of optimism in the main regression, the parameter estimate on the tax rate differential is similar at -0.34 (std. error = 0.15). "Optimistic" households have lower dividend yields relative to households who believe the economy will perform about the same or worse. The parameter estimate on this indicator variable is -0.88 (std. error = 0.37), which is statistically significant at the 5% level.[32]

---

[32]There are other factors that may influence household portfolio dividend yields but are not included because they are endogenous to portfolio choices. The 2003 tax act may have changed where households

33

Several demographic characteristics may have had differential effects on portfolio yields over time. For example, older households may respond differently to a tax change because portfolio choices are influenced by a desire to finance current consumption. To account for this possibility, I run the instrumental variables Tobit model including interaction terms between the age categories and retired indicator variable and the treatment group indicator. In this specification, parameter estimates on the interaction terms are not statistically significantly different from zero, and the estimated tax rate differential effect remains roughly the same.

5.2 Predicted effect of the 2003 Tax Act sunset provisions

The Bush tax cuts of 2001 (the Economic Growth Tax Relief Reconciliation Act of 2001, which reduced ordinary income tax rates for most taxpayers and created a new tax bracket for lowest levels of income) and 2003 are set to expire at the end of 2010. If Congress does not act, dividend income will again be taxed as ordinary income at pre-2001 tax rates and long term capital gains tax rates will increase.[33] I consider the effects of these tax increases implied by the estimates of this study. I simulate marginal and average tax rates that households in the 2007 SCF would face in 2011 by adjusting income variables to 2001 dollars using Consumer Price Index from the Bureau of Labor Statistics and computing tax

locate their dividend-yielding equities, i.e., between taxable or tax-deferred accounts. See Shoven and Sialm (2003) for a discussion of the optimal location of equity securites. Also, concentrated equity holdings in mutual funds may restrict a household's ability to adjust portfolio dividend yields. That these variables are not included may cause bias if the omitted variables are correlated with the included regressors. To check for this possibility, I re-estimate the regression including these additional regressors. Though not presented here, results from these alternative specifications are available upon request from the author. In each, the magnitude of the estimate of the tax rate differential effect remains roughly the same and the parameter estimate on the additional variable is statistically insignificant. These results indicate that excluding these variables is not problematic for interpreting the main estimation results as consistent for the causal effect. There may, of course, remain other factors not considered that make such an interpretation invalid.

[33]Marginal tax rates on dividend income would increase from 15% to 39.6% for those in the highest tax bracket and from 0% to 15% for those in the lowest tax bracket. The top statutory capital gains tax rate will increase from 15% to 20%, and the lowest statutory capital gains tax rates of 0% will increase to 10%.

rates under the 2001 tax rules.[34] For comparison, I first consider the implications of the tax reversals if dividend clientele effects are ignored, i.e., assuming that households do not adjust their equity portfolios (actively or passively) in response to the tax increases. Households in the 2007 SCF received $148 billion in dividend income in 2006 and paid $22.2 billion in taxes on that income.[35] The 2011 average tax rates and dividend receipt patterns in 2007 imply that dividend tax revenue would increase to $38.3 billion in 2011.[36]

This paper shows, however, that households will shift their portfolios away from dividend paying stocks in response to the tax rate increases. Moreover, higher income households will shift away from these stocks by more than lower income households because of their relatively large tax increases. For each household, I compute the change in the dividend and capital gains tax rate differential that they would face in 2011 and the predicted change in portfolio dividend yields.[37] Given the simulated change in dividend and capital gains tax rate differentials and holding the level of equity holdings constant, predicted dividend tax revenues from individuals will only increase to $23.6 billion, less than 62% of the anticipated dividend tax revenues when clientele effects are ignored. If portfolio adjustments are hindered by transaction costs or other adjustment costs, then the increase in dividend tax revenues

---

[34]I compute average dividend tax rates as the ratio of federal income tax liability to federal taxable income, both of which outputs from the TAXSIM model. For households that have negative average tax rates, I treat them as though their average tax rate is zero.

[35]Recall that all summary statistics are weighted by SCF sampling weights and income variables correspond to the calendar year prior to the survey. This level of dividend income, again, is less than the amount reported in the SOI, which reports that $199 billion in ordinary dividends was reported by individuals in 2006.

[36]This exercise holds dividend payout rates constant between 2007 and 2011. There are, however, several reasons to expect that firms will decrease dividend payments. First, Chetty and Saez (2005) find that firms increased dividend payments in response to the 2003 dividend tax cuts. Thus it is likely that firms will decrease dividend payments as dividends become more costly to their investors. This effect is somewhat hindered by evidence of negative investor responses to dividend payment decreases. Secondly, even if total dividend payments do not change, firms will likely accelerate dividend payments to 2010 so that there are lower dividend payments in 2011. Lastly, dividend payouts in 2011 may decrease for nontax reasons. In particular, the financial crisis and recession in the intervening years make profit distributions even less likely.

[37]A household's predicted portfolio dividend yield in 2011 is given by $\widehat{Yield}_{(i,2011)} = Yield_{i,2007} + \hat{\alpha} \cdot \Delta\tau_{(i,2011-2007)} + \hat{\eta}_{2011}$, where $\hat{\alpha}$ is the estimated effect of a 1-percentage point change in the dividend and capital gains tax rate differential, $\Delta\tau_{(i,2011-2007)}$ is the simulated change in the tax rate differential because of the tax rate reversal, and $\hat{\eta}_{2011}$ is a year fixed effect, which would include changes in market prices that result from changes in asset demand. For this simulation, I assume that $\hat{\eta}_{2011} = -\hat{\eta}_{2004}$. That is, average yields are assumed to return to their pre-treatment levels.

could be higher.[38]

5.3 Longer-term response

To understand the longer-term impact of the 2003 tax act, I consider changes to household portfolios between the 2001 and the 2007 Surveys of Consumer Finances. Figure 7 depicts the weighted average portfolio dividend yields for the treatment groups in the 2001, 2004 and 2007 SCF samples. Where there was a large change in portfolio dividend yields immediately following the 2003 tax act, portfolio dividend yields become quite similar across treatment groups by 2007. This is expected. Because the tax treatment of dividends and capital gains is quite similar across households after the 2003 tax act, households should not choose equities based on their dividend payout policies for tax reasons. Results from the instrumental variables Tobit regression model using 2001 and 2007 data are presented in Table 8. The coefficient on the tax rate differential is negative, as expected, but is no longer statistically different from zero. In such a long period, household responses to the 2003 tax act have become diluted so that there is not enough power to detect a tax effect.

Both the descriptive evidence and the econometric estimates provide insight into the nature of household responses to the 2003 tax act. Both sets of information provide evidence that prior to 2003, there was significant variation in household portfolio dividend yields that can be partly explained by differences in tax rates. After a six year window, household portfolio dividend yields become quite similar because the relative tax disadvantage of dividend income for high-income households becomes negligible. This suggests that as households add equities to their portfolios, they are indifferent to dividend payout policies. That is, the incentives to choose particular dividend yields based on taxes no longer exist.

---

[38]Note that dividend tax revenues from other sources should be increasing as individual investors shed their dividend paying stocks and corporations and institutional investors buy them. This paper does not explicitly deal with the effect of dividend tax rates on dividend receipts across different types of investors, necessary for an estimate of how dividend tax revenues from other sources may change in response. If dividend payments are reduced, then even less will be collected in dividend taxes.

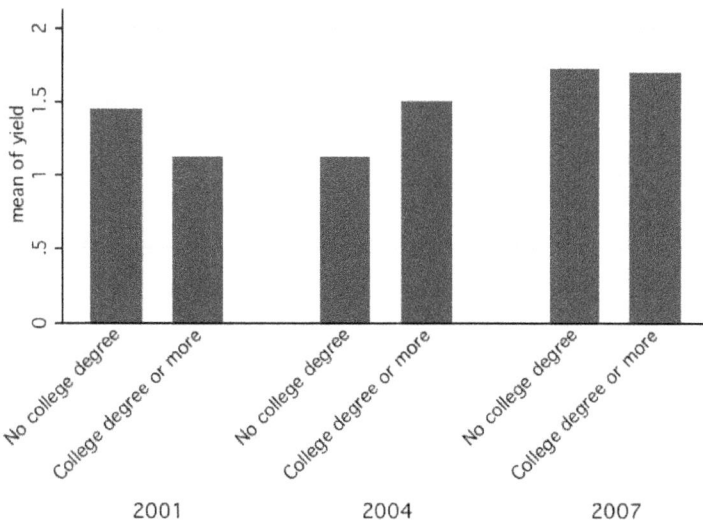

Figure 7: Portfolio dividend yields by educational attainment group: 2001, 2004 and 2007

There are several factors that contribute to the differences between the short-run and longer-run responses to the 2003 tax act. First, increases in firm dividend payments may have been concentrated in firms that were held by high income households, which would inflate high-income households' portfolio dividend yields. Indeed, Chetty and Saez (2005) find evidence that corporations with executives who stood to gain substantially from the dividend tax rate reductions were more likely to initiate or increase dividend payments. Secondly, when the 2003 tax act was first passed, the tax rate reductions were set to expire in 2008. Given the perceived temporary nature of the tax rate reductions, households in the high treatment group may have initially responded by aggressively shifting their portfolios towards high dividend yield stocks. This effect may have dissipated as it became clear that the preferential tax treatment of dividends would last longer.[39] Third, higher income households may have been better informed of the implications of the 2003 tax act on their after-tax portfolio returns. The longer-term response is also consistent with lower income households adjusting their portfolios more slowly. Lastly, the efficiency of capital markets

[39]The Tax Increase Prevention and Reconciliation Act of 2005, enacted on May 17, 2006, prevented several tax provisions, including the reduced dividend and capital gains tax rates, from sunsetting. The lower rates were extended through 2010.

Table 8: Instrumental variables Tobit model, 2001 and 2007

Variable	Estimated Marginal Effect	Std. Error	p-value
Tax differential	-0.07	0.05	0.12
Age 25-35	-0.31	0.57	0.58
Age 35-45	0.14	0.58	0.82
Age 45-55	0.28	0.59	0.63
Age 55-65	0.41	0.6	0.49
Over 65	0.75	0.65	0.25
Retired	-0.09	0.36	0.80
Married	-0.12	0.20	0.54
Household size	-0.25	0.19	0.17
Household size (squared)	0.04	0.04	0.23
College	0.72	0.25	0.00
Net worth 50,000-100,000	0.89	0.46	0.06
Net worth 100,000-250,000	0.73	0.42	0.08
Net worth 250,000-1,000,000	1.56	0.67	0.02
Net worth >1,000,000	2.44	0.93	0.01
Not willing to take financial risk	-1.14	0.36	0.00
Willing to take average financial risk	-0.60	0.27	0.03
Willing to take high financial risk	-0.36	0.29	0.21
SCF = 2007	-0.69	0.66	0.29
Constant	-0.48	0.95	0.61
Number of observations	5810		

Standard errors are computed using the Delta Method and are heteroskedasticity-robust. Observations are weighted by their SCF sampling weights. Estimates are corrected for multiple imputations.

implies that changes in firm dividend policies are immediately capitalized into stock prices. Six years may be too long a period for examining longer-term responses when the equity market adjusts quite quickly. Many other factors may have changed in that period that make it difficult to interpret conditional changes in dividend yields as a tax effect.

5.4 Sensitivity analysis

5.4.1 Model specification and sample selection

I perform a number of sensitivity checks of the main results, which are described in detail in Appendix C. I verify that the magnitude of the dividend and capital gains tax rate differential effect remains unchanged when using more flexible education attainment measures to instrument for marginal tax rates, using alternative cut-points to determine outliers (both to the right and left of the cut-point used in the main analysis), dropping imputed values, and excluding households whose heads are particularly young.

Specification tests for the Tobit model are also provided in Appendix C. As a general diagnostic check, I find that coefficients from a probit model of the household being at the mass point and standardized coefficients from the Tobit model are roughly the same. The Tobit model assumes that the marginal effect of an explanatory variable is the same at both the extensive and intensive margins. To relax this assumption, I estimate a hurdle model which separately estimates the probability of being at the mass point and the relationship between the dependent and explanatory variables for observations away from the mass point. Simulations of the response to the 2003 tax act reveal that the magnitude of the estimated treatment effect is unchanged in this more flexible model.

5.4.2 Alternative explanations for changing dividend demand

A key identifying assumption is that non-tax factors that influence investor preferences for dividends did not change differentially across treatment groups. However, there are several events between 2001 and 2004 that may have influenced preferences. For example, accounting scandals at Enron and PriceWaterhouseCoopers may have led to higher demand for dividends as agency problems were of increasing concern.[40] The effects of such concerns

---

[40]Baker and Wurgler (2004) propose a "catering theory" of dividends, where the salient preferences of investors affect firm dividend payout policies. Interestingly, they reject that taxes influence demands for dividends in favor of other preferences. Relatedly, Becker, Ivkovich and Weisbenner (2009) find that firm

should be capitalized into market prices, and likely do not affect investors differentially. However, if higher income households were relatively more responsive to changes in such non-tax factors, then these changes are included in the estimated tax effect and biases the estimate away from zero (i.e., in favor of finding a dividend clientele effect).

To test whether non-tax preferences for dividends changed differentially across treatment groups, I identify several questions in the SCF about household attitudes that may proxy for non-tax preferences. First, because investors may associate dividends with safety, then risk-averse investors may choose equity portfolios with a higher dividend yield, *ceteris paribus*. To account for changes in risk preferences, I use the risk-averse indicator variable from the main regressions as a dependent variable. To further assess risk preferences, I use a question that asks respondents to choose on a scale from 1 to 5 how strongly they agree with the following statement, "Compared with other people of [my] generation and background, [I] have been lucky in [my] financial affairs." Those who "disagree somewhat" or "disagree strongly" are coded to consider themselves financially unlucky. I posit that those who are not willing to take financial risks and those who believe themselves to be financially unlucky prefer high dividend yield stocks.

Changes in respondents' subjective expectations over the future state of the economy may lead to changes in portfolio choices. Two SCF questions aim to ascertain such beliefs. The first asks, "Over the next five years, do you expect the U.S. economy as a whole to perform better, worse, or about the same as it has over the past five years?" The second asks, "Five years from now, do you think interest rates will be higher, lower, or about the same as today?" From these questions, I construct an indicator variables for whether the household believes the economy will get worse and an indicator variable for whether the household believes that interest rates will increase. For both of these variables, an affirmative response

---

dividend payout policies are related to the age of residents in the headquarters' location. These studies suggest that there is a causal link between the non-tax based dividend preferences of a firm's investors and that firm's payout policy.

is associated with a higher preference for dividends.

To verify that changes to other factors do not confound my estimates, I estimate several probit and linear probability model equations of the following form:

$$preference = \alpha_0 + \alpha_1 college + \alpha_2 college * \mathbb{I}(SCF = 2004) + \alpha_3 \mathbb{I}(SCF = 2004) + X\gamma + u. \quad (11)$$

I construct several dependent variables derived from survey questions that may proxy for non-tax factors that affect the demand for dividends. A test of the null hypothesis that $\alpha_2 = 0$ is a test that underlying preferences did not change for the high treatment group relative to the low treatment group. In each specification, a positive coefficient is posited to be associated with an increase in dividend yields.

Results from these regressions are presented in Table 9, and are quite similar across LPM and probit specifications. In most of these regressions, the parameter estimate on the treatment group is statistically insignificant. The exception is that college educated households are less likely to expect that the economy will become worse. If dividends are associated with safety, this suggests that college educated households would decrease their portfolio dividend yields relative to the low-treatment group. Together, these regressions suggest that non-tax preferences for dividends either did not change, or changed in ways that would bias against finding a dividend clientele effect. However, the included preferences are not directly related to the impact of the accounting scandals and may be inaccurately measured. Additionally, there may also be other factors not considered because they are not available from the survey questions.

Table 9: Regressions for dividend preferences

Dependent variable	Linear Probability Model			Probit		
	$\hat{\alpha}_2$	se($\hat{\alpha}_2$)	p-value	$\hat{\alpha}_2$	se($\hat{\alpha}_2$)	p-value
Economy to get worse in next 5 years	-0.09	0.04	0.02	-0.09	0.04	0.01
Interest rates to be higher in 5 years	0.03	0.04	0.45	0.05	0.04	0.16
Believes unlucky in financial affairs	0.00	0.03	0.95	0.01	0.03	0.75
Not willing to take financial risks	-0.01	0.03	0.68	-0.01	0.02	0.80

Standard errors are heteroskedasticity-robust. Observations are weighted by their SCF sampling weights. Parameter estimates from the probit model reported are average marginal effects. Estimates are corrected for multiple imputations.

5.5 Relationship to previous empirical evidence

This study is not the first to examine the cross-sectional relationship between the tax rate structure and individual portfolio holdings.[41] However, each of the previous studies faces at least one data limitation that makes it unlikely that its estimates are consistent for the causal effect of taxes on household portfolio dividend yields. Few data sources contain detailed information on both marginal tax rates and portfolio structures, and the proxies used likely confound the relationship between taxes and portfolio dividend yields. In addition, most studies use a single cross-section of data which provides estimates of the tax effect that are weakly identified. My analysis avoids these problems to produce a more compelling estimate of the effect of taxes on portfolio dividend yields. The SCF data contain accurate data to compute marginal tax rates and portfolio dividend yields. Using a natural experiment framework, I utilize the plausibly exogenous variation in tax rates to identify tax effects.

Tax return data is limited in the measurement of portfolio dividend yields. Because equity holdings are not reported on tax returns, realized capital gains are used to proxy for equity holdings. Capital gains can be offset against losses and taxes on such gains can be deferred while they accrue, so capital gains realizations are importantly influenced by tax

---

[41]There are cross-sectional studies that find evidence for dividend clienteles within institutional investors. Strickland (1997) finds that taxable institutions exhibit a preference for low-yield stocks, while untaxed institutions such as pension funds do not display any preference with respect to dividend payout policies. Hotchkiss and Lawrence (2003) find a positive relationship between the dividend yield on an equity security and the proportion of a firm's stock held by non-taxable institutional investors.

rates (Feldstein, Slemrod and Yitzhaki 1980). Thus, when trying to isolate the impact of taxes on portfolio dividend yields, the effect of taxes on the timing of capital gains realizations leads to confounding variation in the dependent variable of interest. These results may also be biased if excluded factors not available from tax returns, such as wealth, demographic characteristics and risk preferences, are correlated with tax rates and portfolio choices. Two studies use tax return data and find that, consistent with the dividend clientele hypothesis, dividend yields fall as the marginal tax rate on dividend income rises (Blume, Crockett and Friend (1974), Chaplinsky and Seyhun (1987)).

Brokerage house data contain equity holding information, but marginal tax rate information is limited because individuals report their income only within a small set of ranges. In addition, data from a single firm may not be representative of a household's investments if they hold accounts outside that brokerage house. Two studies use 1960s data on individual portfolio positions from a large national retail brokerage house (Pettit (1977), Lewellen, Stanley, Lease and Schlarbaum (1978)). The limited variation in marginal tax rates along with the differences in empirical methodologies are the likely reasons for their conflicting conclusions drawn from the same data.[42] Graham and Kumar (2006) use 1990s brokerage house data and find that the relationship between income and portfolios is consistent with the dividend clientele hypothesis. Examining stock holding patterns around the Revenue Reconciliation Act of 1993, they document that changes to dividend yields across income groups are consistent with tax-based dividend clienteles. While they provide the only other study to use a natural experiment, they cannot distinguish tax effects from income effects.

Scholz (1992) uses the 1983 SCF so, like my study, is able to accurately compute marginal tax rates and portfolio dividend yields. He finds that the relationship between tax rates and portfolio dividend yields supports dividend clientele effects.[43] There are limitations to using

---

[42]Pettit uses a linear regression model and finds evidence for a clientele effect, whereas Lewellen, et al. use linear discriminant analysis and conclude there is not sufficient evidence to support the dividend clientele hypothesis.

[43]Scholz (1994) provides descriptive evidence for dividend clienteles by examining portfolio dividend yields

a single cross-section to study tax effects, however, as explained in section 5. In addition, the tax rate instrument used, the rate assuming that all households have the same portfolio dividend yield, is endogenous if households simultaneously make choices over labor and investment income.[44] He estimates a large effect of taxes on portfolio dividend yields that is three times larger than that found in this study, a magnitude that may be implausibly large (Poterba 2002).[45]

To compare my estimates to Scholz (1992) and better understand the gains from using a natural experiments framework, I estimate my model using each SCF cross-section separately. Because the high-treatment indicator variable is no longer available as an instrument, I use an instrument based off of the tax rates that apply to the "first dollar" of investment income.[46] These results are presented in Table 15 in Appendix C, where they are also described in greater detail. The estimated magnitude of the tax effect is much smaller when using a single cross-section, and is no longer statistically significantly different from zero when using the 2004 SCF. Together, these findings are consistent with the weaker identification of the tax effect using a single cross-section, and suggest that the instrument used when estimating on a single cross-section is endogenous. The difference in magnitude found in Scholz's (1992) study also reflects the relative prevalence of dividends as a means distributing profits to shareholders in the 1980's.

Two studies test for dividend clienteles using the 2003 tax acts. Both of these studies focus

---

by income decile and by marginal tax rate ranges in two SCF samples around the Tax Reform Act of 1986. He provides tabulations that show that households in the highest ranges of the income distribution have below-average dividend yields.

[44]The direction of bias from using this instrument is ambiguous because it depends on the relationship between labor and investment income. Absent substitution effects between dividend and non-dividend income, the tax rate will fall for marginal individuals who reduce their dividend income to reduce their tax liabilities. This would cause an upward bias in the estimated tax effect.

[45]Scholz concludes that moving from a system with no taxes to a one with a 50-percent marginal tax rate, portfolio dividend yields are predicted to increase by 5.4 percentage points. This simulation is difficult to interpret because we should expect that when tax rates are similar across households, there are no tax-based dividend clienteles.

[46]This is equivalent to the instrument in Scholz (1992) if portfolio yields are assumed to be zero. The results do not change substantively if the instrument is constructed assuming that all households receive the average yield on their portfolios.

Table 10: Instrumental variables Tobit on single cross-sections

	2001			2004		
Variable	Est. Marg. Effect	Std. Error	p-value	Est. Marg. Effect	Std. Error	p-value
Tax differential	-0.03	0.02	0.09	0.00	0.03	0.97
Age 25-35	2.52	1.20	0.04	1.54	1.06	0.15
Age 35-45	2.61	1.27	0.04	1.48	1.13	0.19
Age 45-55	3.04	1.41	0.03	1.81	1.26	0.15
Age 55-65	3.00	1.30	0.02	1.57	1.17	0.18
Over 65	3.33	1.43	0.02	2.23	1.37	0.10
Retired	0.19	0.48	0.70	0.10	0.40	0.80
Married	0.07	0.51	0.89	-0.46	0.31	0.13
Household size	-0.61	0.33	0.07	-0.21	0.30	0.47
Household size (squared)	0.07	0.07	0.30	0.02	0.05	0.66
College	0.73	0.36	0.04	0.64	0.31	0.04
Net worth 50,000-100,000	0.23	1.19	0.85	0.44	0.85	0.61
Net worth 100,000-250,000	0.18	0.94	0.84	0.75	0.71	0.29
Net worth 250,000-1,000,000	1.41	1.03	0.17	1.60	0.83	0.06
Net worth >1,000,000	2.19	1.08	0.04	2.48	0.83	0.00
Not willing to take financial risk	-0.64	0.54	0.23	-0.68	0.36	0.06
Constant	-4.38	0.55	0.00	-4.00	0.63	0.00
F-statistic on instrument	852.77			626.61		

Standard errors are heteroskedasticity-robust. Observations are weighted by their SCF sampling weights. Parameter estimates from the probit model reported are average marginal effects. Estimates are corrected for multiple imputations.

on changes to individual equity holding patterns in the aggregate rather than differential changes in equity holding patterns across individual investors, which is done in this paper. Desai and Dharmapala (2007) exploit that the 2003 tax act lowered the tax treatment on dividends from US firms and only extended this preferential treatment to a subset of foreign firms. They estimate the impact of the tax policy change on US investor equity holdings in affected and unaffected countries and find a large response to the 2003 tax act. Blouin, Raedy and Shackelford (2010) examine the relationship between changes in dividend payout policies and changes in equity holding patterns among insiders, mutual funds, and individual investors. They find that firm executives, but not other individual investors, rebalanced their equity portfolios in response to the dividend tax cuts. Because they collapse individual investor holdings (as the number of shares outstanding less the shares held by insiders and mutual funds), their result does not necessarily contradict the findings in this study.

Another approach to studying the dividend clientele hypothesis uses stock price movements or trade volumes to infer the tax-based preferences of stock market participants. This literature compares changes in the share price of an equity on the day in which investors are no longer eligible to receive a previously declared dividend, the "ex-dividend day", with the value of the dividend payment to infer the relative after-tax valuation of dividends and capital gains. This approach is quite different from that used in this study, but is briefly reviewed in Appendix B for completeness. Overall, these studies have provided mixed results regarding the dividend clientele hypothesis.

6 Conclusion

The empirical results presented in this paper strongly support the dividend clientele hypothesis. When there is significant cross-sectional variation in dividend and capital gains tax rates prior to the 2003 tax act, dividend clienteles emerge as individuals rationally seek the highest post-tax return on their portfolios. Exploiting the exogenous variation in dividend and capital gains tax rates provided by the Jobs and Growth Tax Relief Reconciliation Act of 2003, the relationship between changes in portfolio dividends yields and changes in tax rates reveals a statistically significant dividend clientele effect. This analysis also provides evidence that household responses to the 2003 tax act were economically significant. Because of dividend clienteles, changes in tax rates induced by the 2003 tax act caused a 0.94 percentage point differential change in portfolio dividend yield between high and low treatment groups. Numerous sensitivity checks are performed to check model misspecification and to confirm that these changes in portfolio dividend yields are not explained by other factors, such as changes to investor optimism or risk aversion.

This paper contributes to the existing literature that examines the existence of tax-based dividend clienteles both in terms of the econometric methodology employed and in the quality of data used. Utilizing a natural experiments framework provides a more precise estimate of the dividend clientele effect than previous studies, which generally rely on variation in a single cross-section of data. This plausibly exogenous variation in tax schedules allows for a consistent estimate of the causal effect of taxes on household choices over portfolio dividend yields. The Survey of Consumer Finances provides detailed information on household equity portfolios and marginal tax rates. This allows for a direct test of the relationship between tax rates and portfolio dividend yields, rather than providing suggestive evidence derived from correlations or inaccurately measured variables.

Because high-income households have historically received a significant proportion of dividends paid, affluent households benefitted from significant reductions in tax liabilities because of the 2003 tax act. In addition, shifts towards high dividend-paying stocks by high-income households imply that even larger tax benefits accrued to high-income households as a result of the 2003 tax act. Accounting for clientele effects is important for understanding the distributional consequences of changes to tax rates on investment income. In particular, these findings suggest that ignoring dividend clientele effects will cause estimates of the elasticity of taxable income with respect to capital tax rates to be biased.

There are limitations to this study that suggest avenues for future research. First, because I do not have panel data that contains information on the specific stocks in household equity portfolios, I am unable to separately identify active and passive portfolio rebalancing. Brokerage account data may aide in answering this question, though it would likely not include marginal tax rate information. Second, differences between the short-term and long-term responses to the 2003 tax act provide interesting insights into the nature of portfolio adjustments. Better understanding how investors internalize new information about the tax implications of their portfolio choices is an interesting extension for understanding responses to the 2003 tax act. Lastly, there may be other clienteles in the market that are important for a complete analysis of the effect of taxes on portfolio choices over dividend yields. For example, many institutional investors, a growing proportion of investors, are tax exempt and so may form another dividend clientele. To better understand the overall impact of the 2003 tax act, future work should be done to assess the impact of the tax act on institutional investors' portfolios. In addition, this paper focuses on clientele effects within equity portfolios. There may be other tax-based clienteles that form across other financial assets.

A Review of market-based approaches

When investors have heterogeneous after-tax valuations of dividends and capital gains, they may adjust their trading behavior around ex-dividend days to capture or avoid upcoming dividend payments. Such adjustments imply that a share's price drop around its ex-dividend day relative to the dividend payment is related to the tax rates of its investors, controlling for other market fluctuations. If tax-based dividend clienteles exist, then the tax rates implied by these price changes will differ across equities according to their dividend yields.

Using this intuition, Elton and Gruber (1970) derive a test for dividend clienteles and find strong evidence for the existence of dividend clienteles. Since Elton and Gruber's (1970) seminal study, over one hundred articles regarding ex-dividend pricing behaviors have been published, with mixed results. An incomplete list of studies includes: Litzenberger and Ramaswamy (1979) Litzenberger and Ramaswamy (1980), Litzenberger and Ramaswamy (1982) and Auerbach (1983), that find evidence in favor of dividend clienteles, and Black and Scholes (1974), and Gordon and Bradford (1980), Miller and Scholes (1982), and Michaely (1991) that find they cannot reject the null hypothesis that dividends and capital gains are valued equally.

While the ex-dividend day studies may summarize the impact of taxes on aggregate market behavior, they do not identify a direct link between investor behavior and taxes, which would require micro-level data on stock holdings and tax rates. In addition, interpreting these ex-dividend day results are complicated by several factors. First, the coincidence of ex-dividend days and dividend announcement days may lead to a spurious correlation between returns and dividend yields (Miller and Scholes (1982), Gordon and Bradford (1980)). Second, the interpretation of the ex-dividend studies depends on whether a stock's "typical" investors are setting prices around ex-dividend days. If price changes are driven by short-term investors, the price movements contain little information about the characteristics of a firm's long-term investors. The return on a stock may be a function of the interactions between multiple classes of investors, so it is difficult to obtain information about clienteles from market price movements (Michaely and Vila 1995). Finally, these studies do not account for transaction costs or risk aversion because they are not available from stock market data.

B Sensitivity analysis

B.1 Alternative instruments

The discretization of tax treatment intensity by an indicator for whether the household head has a college degree may be too stark. To allow a more flexible relationship between education level and tax rates, I construct additional educational attainment measures based on years of schooling and whether the household head earned a high school degree. Similar to the main specification, the instruments for a household's tax rate are the interactions of the educational attainment measures and an indicator variable for whether the observation comes from the 2004 SCF sample.

Table 11 presents the estimated tax effect from the instrumental variables Tobit model using these alternative instruments, along with the F-statistic on the instrument(s) from the first-stage regressions. The specification with three educational attainment categories distinguishes households according to whether household heads have a high school degree or less, some college education but no college degree, and a college degree. The specification with four categories additionally distinguishes those households in which the head has a high school degree or equivalent from those in which the household head has no degree. Years of schooling is also used as an alternative instrument. This additional flexibility for determining the intensity of tax treatment does not much change the estimates of the tax effect from the main results. Differentiating households by whether the head has a college degree approximates differences in marginal tax rates quite well, at least for that on investment income.

In addition, to purge the estimates of the effect of individuals who had not yet completed their education, I run the main regression including only households whose heads are at least 35 years old. Whether the household head has a college degree is the instrument used. Estimates from this specification are also presented in Table 11.

Table 11: Results using alternative instruments and samples

| | Tax rate differential | | | |
Instrument(s)	Est. Marg. Effect	Std. Error	p-value	First-stage F-statistic
Three education categories	-0.35	0.15	0.02	15.54
Four education categories	-0.28	0.13	0.04	10.65
Years of schooling	-0.26	0.12	0.02	24.05
				No. obs. dropped
Head over 30 years old	-0.28	0.14	0.05	180

The top panel presents select results from instrumental variable Tobit regressions using alternative instruments for the dividend and capital gain tax rate differential. The bottom panel presents select results when excluding households with a head less than 30 years of age.

B.2 Outliers and Imputed Values

In the main estimation, nine observations are dropped because their portfolio dividend yields are greater than 1000%. To analyze the sensitivity of the analysis to outliers, I re-estimate the model using other cut-points. The results from these estimations are provided in Table 12, with the main results in the middle row for comparison. Except for the most extreme outliers, the estimates are not sensitive to the choice of cut-off points. To check that the estimates are not sensitive to imputed values, I run regressions excluding households whose dividend income or at least one component of taxable equities were missing in the original data file. This excludes 512 observations from the 2001 SCF sample and 320 observations from the 2004 SCF sample, and omits a disproportionate number of households whose heads did not earn a college degree. Results using this selected sample are similar to the main results.

B.3 Tobit model assumptions and alternative models

As a general specification test of the Tobit model, I compare the coefficients from a probit model for being at the mass point with the coefficients from the Tobit model standardized by the estimated standard deviation of the model errors. These estimates are presented in

Table 12: Results using different cut-offs for outliers and excluding imputed values

	Tax differential			No. of obs. deleted
	Est. Marg. Effect	Std. Error	p-value	
Include all observations	-0.97	0.78	0.21	0
Drop if yield > 2000	-1.16	0.63	0.07	6
Drop if yield > 1500	-0.29	0.15	0.06	7
Drop if yield > 1000	-0.31	0.14	0.03	9
Drop if yield > 500	-0.30	0.14	0.03	11
Drop if yield > 300	-0.28	0.12	0.02	14
Drop imputed values	-0.32	0.13	0.01	717

This table presents select results from instrumental variable Tobit regressions using different samples based on changing cut-offs for outliers and by dropping imputed values.

Table 13. A general test of whether the Tobit model is mis-specified is done by comparing these coefficients. The estimated coefficients are all of the same sign, as expected. They are also generally similar in magnitude, except for the net worth categories.

The Tobit model restricts the effect of the explanatory variables to be the same for both the extensive margin of whether to receive dividends and the intensive margin of the portfolio dividend yield. To relax this assumption, I run a hurdle model that separately estimates a probit model for having a positive dividend yield and an instrumental variables regression of dividend yields on the uncensored observations. To help account for heteroskedasticity in portfolio dividend yields, the dependent variable in the instrumental variables regression is the log of a household's portfolio dividend yield. Results from the hurdle model are presented in Table 14.

That most coefficients are of the same sign indicates that the variables have the same directional effect on both the decision to receive dividends and the choice over dividend yields. The exceptions are the indicator variable for being retired (though not statistically different from zero) and the net worth categories. Interestingly, the tax rate differential effect is five times larger in the instrumental variables regression than in the probit model. Moreover, it is statistically significant at the 10% level in the instrumental variables regression, but

53

Table 13: Comparing probit and standardized Tobit estimates

Variable	Est. Coeff. from Probit	Std. Coeff. from Tobit
Tax differential	-0.03	-0.05
Age 25-35	0.52	0.65
Age 35-45	0.51	0.75
Age 45-55	0.60	0.89
Age 55-65	0.56	0.85
Over 65	0.64	0.82
Retired	0.13	-0.13
Married	-0.04	-0.04
Household size	-0.12	-0.08
Household size (squared)	0.01	0.01
College	0.35	0.31
Net worth 50,000-100,000	0.27	-0.06
Net worth 100,000-250,000	0.38	0.01
Net worth 250,000-1,000,000	0.89	0.43
Net worth >1,000,000	1.50	0.84
Not willing to take financial risk	-0.41	-0.30
Willing to take average financial risk	-0.09	-0.06
Willing to take high financial risk	0.09	0.01
SCF = 2004	-0.35	-0.67
Constant	-0.92	-0.52

Coefficients from the Tobit model are standardized by the estimated standard deviation of the error term. Observations are weighted by their SCF sampling weights. Parameter estimates are corrected for multiple imputations.

not significantly different from zero in the probit model. This suggests that taxes may be important for determining dividend yields at the intensive margin rather than at the extensive margin. Thus, shifts to dividend clienteles caused by the 2003 tax act are likely confined to shifts among clienteles with some dividend income, rather than inducing more households to receive dividends.

Simulations of the impact of the 2003 tax act on household portfolio dividend yields produce similar results to those generated by the instrumental variables Tobit model. The high-treatment (college educated) group is predicted to increase its portfolio dividend yield by 4.53 percentage points while the low-treatment (non-college educated) group is predicted

Table 14: Hurdle model for household portfolio dividend yields

	Probit			IV Regression		
Dependent variable:	Indicator for yield > 0			Log Dividend Yield		
	Est	Std.		Est	Std.	
Variable	Coeff	Error	p-value	Coeff	Error	p-value
Tax differential	-0.02	0.03	0.53	-0.11	0.06	0.09
Age 25-35	0.49	0.25	0.05	0.73	0.53	0.17
Age 35-45	0.48	0.26	0.06	1.03	0.53	0.05
Age 45-55	0.57	0.25	0.03	1.09	0.51	0.03
Age 55-65	0.50	0.25	0.04	1.20	0.51	0.02
Over 65	0.58	0.27	0.03	1.25	0.54	0.02
Retired	0.14	0.19	0.44	-0.36	0.26	0.17
Married	-0.03	0.10	0.76	-0.29	0.31	0.34
Household size	-0.16	0.10	0.10	-0.11	0.37	0.76
Household size (squared)	0.02	0.01	0.13	0.03	0.05	0.62
College	0.36	0.09	0.00	0.53	0.27	0.05
Net worth 50,000-100,000	0.33	0.16	0.04	-0.73	0.53	0.17
Net worth 100,000-250,000	0.41	0.14	0.00	-1.05	0.45	0.02
Net worth 250,000-1,000,000	0.91	0.18	0.00	-0.76	0.51	0.13
Net worth >1,000,000	1.49	0.28	0.00	-0.39	0.66	0.56
Not willing to take financial risk	-0.36	0.11	0.00	-0.27	0.29	0.35
SCF = 2004	-0.33	0.37	0.38	-1.49	0.79	0.06
Number of observations		3956			2379	

Standard errors are heteroskedasticity-robust. Observations are weighted by their SCF sampling weights. Estimates from the probit model are average marginal effects. Estimates are corrected for multiple imputations.

to increase by 3.25 percentage points. Thus, there is an estimated 1.28 percentage point differential increase across treatment groups. The more flexible model provides very similar results to the Tobit model.

B.4 Analysis using single cross-sections

Results from regressions based on a single SCF cross-section are provided in Table 15. The components for the instrumental variable for tax rates are computed using TAXSIM. Specifically, I compute the marginal tax rate that applies to a household's last dollar of taxable income less capital gains, dividend income and interest income. The difference in these dividend and capital gains marginal tax rates are used to instrument for the actual dividend and capital gain marginal tax rate differential.

Table 15: Instrumental variables Tobit on single cross-sections

| | 2001 | | | 2004 | | |
Variable	Est. Marg. Effect	Std. Error	p-value	Est. Marg. Effect	Std. Error	p-value
Tax differential	-0.03	0.02	0.09	0.00	0.03	0.97
Age 25-35	2.52	1.20	0.04	1.54	1.06	0.15
Age 35-45	2.61	1.27	0.04	1.48	1.13	0.19
Age 45-55	3.04	1.41	0.03	1.81	1.26	0.15
Age 55-65	3.00	1.30	0.02	1.57	1.17	0.18
Over 65	3.33	1.43	0.02	2.23	1.37	0.10
Retired	0.19	0.48	0.70	0.10	0.40	0.80
Married	0.07	0.51	0.89	-0.46	0.31	0.13
Household size	-0.61	0.33	0.07	-0.21	0.30	0.47
Household size (squared)	0.07	0.07	0.30	0.02	0.05	0.66
College	0.73	0.36	0.04	0.64	0.31	0.04
Net worth 50,000-100,000	0.23	1.19	0.85	0.44	0.85	0.61
Net worth 100,000-250,000	0.18	0.94	0.84	0.75	0.71	0.29
Net worth 250,000-1,000,000	1.41	1.03	0.17	1.60	0.83	0.06
Net worth >1,000,000	2.19	1.08	0.04	2.48	0.83	0.00
Not willing to take financial risk	-0.64	0.54	0.23	-0.68	0.36	0.06
Constant	-4.38	0.55	0.00	-4.00	0.63	0.00
F-statistic on instrument	852.77			626.61		

Standard errors are heteroskedasticity-robust. Observations are weighted by their SCF sampling weights. Parameter estimates from the probit model reported are average marginal effects. Estimates are corrected for multiple imputations.

Using the 2001 SCF cross-section provides a much smaller, though still negative, estimate of the tax effect on portfolio dividend yields that is only statistically significant at the 10% level. As with the main results, I simulate the predicted impact of the 2003 tax act on portfolio dividend yields. Using these simulated changes to portfolio dividend yields, the average impact of the tax act between the college-educated and non-college-educated group is also much smaller. College-educated households are predicted to increase their yields by 0.41 percentage points, whereas non-college-educated households are predicted to increase their yields by 0.32 percentage points. The single cross-section analysis would lead us to conclude that taxes have a much smaller impact on portfolio dividend yields than the analysis using a natural experiment suggests. The estimated tax effect using the 2004 SCF cross-section is not statistically different from zero. This is likely because tax rates becomes much more homogeneous after the 2003 tax act leading to insufficient cross-sectional variation in the tax rate variable.

Overall, estimating tax effects with a single cross-section provides a very different picture of the dividend clientele effect and depends strongly on the cross-sectional variation of tax rates in the period considered. Even when there is larger cross-sectional variation in the 2001 tax rate differential, identification is much weaker than in a natural experiments framework. In addition, using the potentially endogenous tax rate instrument may bias the estimates. When the dividend tax rate is reduced to the capital gains tax rate, households may respond by switching some labor income towards dividend income. The resulting bias in the estimated coefficients is ambiguous, as it depends on the relative changes in tax rates and dividend yields.

References

Allen, F., A. Bernardo, and I. Welch, "A theory of dividends based on tax clienteles," *Journal of Finance*, 2000, *LV* (6).

Amemiya, T., "The estimation of a simultaneous-equation generalized probit model ," *Econometrica*, 1978, *46*.

———, "The estimation of a simultaneous-equation Tobit model ," *International Economic Review*, 1979, *20*.

Antoniewicz, R., "A comparison of the household sector from the Flow of Funds Accounts and the Survey of Consumer Finances," 1996. FEDS Working paper No. 96-26.

Auerbach, A., "Stockholder tax rates and firm attributes," *Journal of Public Economics*, 1983, *21*.

——— **and K. Hassett**, "The 2003 dividend tax cuts and the value of the firm: An event study," in A. Auerbach, J. Hines, and J. Slemrod, eds., *Taxing corporate income in the 21st century*, Cambridge University Press, 2007.

——— **and M. King**, "Taxation, portfolio choice, and debt-equity ratios: A general equilibrium model," *Quarterly Journal of Economics*, Nov 1983, *98* (4).

Baker, M. and J. Wurgler, "A catering theory of dividends," *The Journal of Finance*, Nov 2004, *59* (3).

Becker, B., Z. Ivkovich, and S. Weisbenner, "Local dividend clienteles," *NBER Working Paper 15175*, July 2009.

Bernheim, B., "Tax policy and the dividend puzzle," *The RAND Journal of Economics*, 1991, *22* (4).

Bhattacharya, S., "Imperfect information, dividend policy, and 'the bird in the hand' fallacy," *The Bell Journal of Economics*, 1979, *1*.

Black, F. and M. Scholes, "The effects of dividend yield and dividend policy on common stock prices and returns," *Journal of FInancial Economics*, 1974.

Blouin, J., J. Raedy, and D. Shackelford, "Dividends, share repurchases and tax clienteles: Evidence from the 2003 reductions in shareholder taxes," 2010. NBER Working Paper 16129.

Blume, M., E. Crockett, and I. Friend, "Stockholders in the United States: Characteristics and trends," *Survey of Current Business*, 1974.

Blundell, R., A. Duncan, and C. Meghir, "Estimating labor supply responses using tax reforms," *Econometrica*, 1998, *87*.

Brav, A., J. Graham, C. Harvey, and R. Michaely, "Payout policy in the 21st century," *Journal of Financial Economics*, 2005, *77*.

Brennan, M., "Taxes, market valuation and corporate financial policy," *National Tax Journal*, 1970, *25*.

Brown, J., N. Liang, and S. Weisbenner, "Executive financial incentives and payout policy: Firm responses to the 2003 dividend tax cut," *FEDS Working Paper 2006-14*, 2004.

Bucks, B., A. Kennickell, and K. Moore, "Recent changes in U.S. family finances: Evidence from the 2001 and 2004 Surveys of Consumer Finances," *Federal Reserve Bulletin*, 2006.

Cameron, A.C. and P. Trivedi, *Microeconomics methods and applications*, Cambridge University Press, 2006.

Chaplinsky, S. and H. Seyhun, "Tax rationality and the demand for dividends," 1987. Working Paper, University of Michigan.

Chetty, R. and E. Saez, "Dividend taxes and corporate behavior: Evidence from the 2003 dividend tax cut," *Quarterly Journal of Economics*, August 2005, *CXX* (3).

Desai, M. and D. Dharmapala, "Taxes and portfolio choice: Evidence from JGTRRA's treatment of international dividends," *NBER Working Paper No. 13281*, July 2007.

Eissa, N., "Labor supply and the Economic Recovery Tax Reform of 1981," in M. Feldstein and J. Poterba, eds., *Empirical Foundations of Household Taxation*, Chicago, 1996.

_____ , "Tax reforms and labor supply," in J. Poterba, ed., *Tax Policy and the Economy*, Vol. 10, MIT Press, 1996.

Elton, E. and M. Gruber, "Marginal stockholder tax rates and the clientele effect," *Review of Economics and Statistics*, 1970, *52*.

Feenberg, D. and E. Coutts, "An introduction to the TAXSIM model," *Journal of Policy Analysis and Management*, 1993, *12* (1).

Feldstein, M., J. Slemrod, and S. Yitzhaki, "The effects of taxation on the selling of corporate stock and the realization of capital gains," *Quarterly Journal of Economics*, 1980, *94* (1).

Galper, H., R. Lucke, and E. Toder, "A general equilibrium analysis of tax reform," in H. Aaron, H. Galper, and J. Pechman, eds., *Uneasy compromise: Problems of a hybrid income-consumption tax*, Brookings, 1988.

Gordon, R. and D. Bradford, "Taxation and the stock market valuation of capital gains and dividends," *Journal of Public Economics*, 1980, *14*.

Graham, J. and A. Kumar, "Do dividend clienteles exist? Evidence on dividend preferences for retail investors," *Journal of Finance*, 2006, *LXI* (3).

Hamada, R. and M. Scholes, "Taxes and corporate financial management," in E. Altman and M. Subrahmanyam, eds., *Recent Advances in Corporate Finance*, Richard Irwin, 1985.

Heckman, J., "Comment on N. Eissa Labor supply and the Economic Recovery Tax Reform of 1981," in M. Feldstein and J. Poterba, eds., *Empirical Foundations of Household Taxation*, Chicago, 1996.

___ **and R. Robb**, "Alternative methods for evaluating the impact of interventions," in J. Heckman and B. Singer, eds., *Longitudinal Analysis of Labor Market Data*, Cambridge University Press, 1985.

Hotchkiss, E. and S. Lawrence, "Empirical evidence on the existence of dividend clienteles," 2003. Working paper, Department of Finance, Boston College.

Ivkovic, Z., J. Poterba, and S. Weisbenner, "Tax-motivated trading by individual investors," *The American Economic Review*, 2005, *95* (5).

Jensen, M. and W. Meckling, "Theory of the firm: Managerial behavior, agency costs and ownership structure," *Journal of Financial Economics*, 1976, *3*.

Kennickell, A., "Multiple imputation in the Survey of Consumer Finances," *Board of Governors of the Federal Reserve System*, 1998.

Kezdi, G. and R. Willis, "Who becomes a stockholder? Expectations, subjective uncertainty, and asset allocation," 2003. Working Paper, University of Michigan Retirement Research Center.

King, M. and D. Fullerton, *The Taxation of Income from Capital*, The University of Chicago Press, 1984.

— and J. Leape, "Wealth and portfolio composition: Theory and evidence," *Journal of Public Economics*, 1998, *69*.

Leape, J., "Taxes and transaction costs in asset market equilibrium," *Journal of Public Economics*, 1987, *33*.

Lewellen, W., K. Stanley, R. Lease, and G. Schlarbaum, "Some direct evidence on the dividend clientele phenomenon," *Journal of Finance*, 1978, *33*.

Lightner, T., M. Morrow, R. Ricketts, and M. Riley, "Investor response to a reduction in the dividend tax rate: Evidence from the Jobs and Growth Tax Relief Reconciliation Act of 2003," *Journal of the American Taxation Association*, Fall 2008.

Litzenberger, R. and K. Ramaswamy, "The effect of personal taxes and dividends on capital asset prices: Theory and empirical evidence," *Journal of Financial Economics*, Fall 1979, *7*.

— and — , "Dividends, short selling restrictions, tax-induced investor clienteles and market equilibrium," *Journal of Finance*, May 1980, *35* (2).

— and — , "The effects of dividends on common stock prices: Tax effects or information effects?," *Journal of Finance*, 1982, *37*.

Long, J., "Efficient portfolio choice with differential taxation of dividends and capital gains," *Journal of Financial Economics*, May 1977.

Michaely, R., "Ex-dividend day stock price behavior: The case of the 1986 Tax Reform Act," *The Journal of Finance*, July 1991, *46* (3).

62

____ **and J. Vila**, "Investors' heterogeneity, prices, and volume around the ex-dividend day," *Journal of Financial and Quantitative Analysis*, 1995, *30*.

Miller, M., "Debt and taxes," *Journal of Finance*, 1977, *32*.

____ **and F. Modigliani**, "Dividend policy, growth, and the valuation of shares," *Journal of Business*, 1961.

____ **and M. Scholes**, "Dividends and taxes: Some empirical evidence," *Journal of Political Economy*, 1982, *90*.

Modigliani, F. and M. Miller, "The cost of capital, corporation finance and the theory of investment," *American Economic Review*, 1958.

Moffitt, R. and M. Wilhelm, "Taxation and labor supply decisions of the affluent," in J. Slemrod, ed., *Does Atlas Shrug? The Economic Consequences of Taxing the Rich*, Russell Sage Foundation and Harvard University Press, 2000.

Newey, W., "Efficient estimation of limited dependent variable models with endogenous explanatory variables," *Journal of Econometrics*, 1987, *36*.

Pettit, R., "Taxes, transactions costs and the clientele effect of dividends," *Journal of Financial Economics*, 1977.

Poterba, J., "Taxation, risk-taking, and household portfolio behavior," in A. Auerbach and M. Feldstein, eds., *Handbook of Public Economics*, Vol. 3, Russell Sage Foundation and Harvard University Press, 2002.

____ **and A. Samwick**, "Taxation and household portfolio composition: US evidence from the 1980s and 1990s," *Journal of Public Economics*, 2002.

Scholz, J. K., "A direct examination of the dividend clientele hypothesis," *Journal of Public Economics*, 1992, *49*.

____ , "Tax progressivity and household portfolios," in J. Slemrod, ed., *Tax Progressivity and Income Inequality*, Cambridge University Press, 1994.

Shefrin, H. and M. Statman, "Explaining investor preference for cash dividends," *Journal of Financial Economics*, 1984, *13*.

____ **and R. Thaler**, "The behavioral life-cycle hypothesis," *Economic Inquiry*, 1988, *26*.

Shoven, J. and C. Sialm, "Asset location in tax-deferred and conventional savings accounts," *Journal of Public Economics*, 2003, *88*.

Smith, R. and R. Blundell, "An exogeneity test for a simultaneous equation Tobit model with an application to labor supply," *Econometrica*, 1986.

Stock, J. and M. Yogo, "Testing for weak instruments in linear IV regression," Nov 2002. NBER Working Paper No. T0284.

Strickland, D., "Determinants of institutional ownership: Implications for dividend clienteles," 1997. Working paper, Ohio State University.

Wooldridge, J., *Econometric analysis of cross section and panel data*, Massachusetts Institute of Technology, 2002.

www.ingramcontent.com/pod-product-compliance
Lightning Source LLC
Chambersburg PA
CBHW052011280526
45793CB00005B/937